13.95

D0114688

# Parishes
# That Excel

# Patrick J. Brennan

# Parishes
# That Excel

Models of Excellence in
Education, Ministry, and Evangelization

CROSSROAD • NEW YORK

1992

The Crossroad Publishing Company
370 Lexington Avenue, New York, NY 10017

Copyright © 1992 by Patrick J. Brennan

Printed in the United States of America

**Library of Congress Cataloging-in-Publication Data**

Brennan, Patrick J.
    Parishes that excel : models of excellence in education, ministry, and evangelization / Patrick J. Brennan.
        p.    cm.
    ISBN 0-8245-1156-5
    1. Pastoral theology—United States—Case studies.    2. Pastoral theology—Catholic Church—Case studies.    3. Catholic Church—Middle West—Membership.    4. Parishes—Middle West—Case studies.
I. Title.
BV4011.B66    1992
250'.973—dc20                                                            92-1208
                                                                          CIP

*To K.C. and her little sister,*
*little meteors of God's love*
*who have reminded me of the need*
*for Sabbath time*

# Contents

# Preface

In serving as the director of the Office for Chicago Catholic Evangelization, I have been blessed with relationships with many committed pastoral ministers working on and shaping excellent models of evangelization, education, and pastoral ministry in the Midwest. In another role, president of the National Center for Evangelization and Parish Renewal, I have had my consciousness expanded to include models of excellence in other parts of the country. The stories, models, and leaders discussed in this book in no way include all the excellent parishes that I have encountered. They are but a sampling, exhibiting excellence in areas that I consider cutting-edge issues for the future: inculturation, young adult ministry, evangelization, reach-out, catechetical renewal, small Christian communities, family perspective. I am indebted to all the people and places here who have helped me grow in wisdom. I am deeply grateful again to Dawn Mayer Melendez, long-time friend and colleague, for her critique and final editorial assistance.

# CHAPTER ONE

# Excellence

---

Several years ago, I began to be quite impressed with the books and regular newsletter of Tom Peters and his associates. His wisdom has been captured in *In Search of Excellence, A Passion for Excellence*, and *Thriving on Chaos*, his newsletters on excellence, and his video presentations on public television and elsewhere. Though he is writing about business corporations and serving customers, I have always found his material quite adaptable for church purposes and serving parishioners. To deal with this question, he graciously accepted an invitation to come to Chicago and talk to a group of parishioners and church leaders on excellence in service. It was wonderful to see the number of ordinary believers, the lay people, the *laos theou*, who came to learn about excellence in service. It was sad to see how few of the clergy and hierarchy were present. Even after Mr. Peters offered free consultation time, the Notre Dame game that Saturday was seemingly more important than learning about excellence.

What Tom Peters confronts in an ailing American economy is what Diane Fassell and Ann Wilson Schaef address in their work on addictive organizations. In *When Society Becomes an Addict* and *The Addictive Organization* they speak of the mass-mindedness of so many within society and organizations, frozen and clinging to structures that no longer fit the mission. More recently Stephen Covey has said similar things in *The Seven Habits of Highly Effective People;* he speaks of the need for people and organizations to articulate their mission, but also to determine what they must say yes to and what they must say no to in order to complete that mission. I adapted these principles and concerns to parish work in *Re-Imagining the Parish*, in which I spoke of the church as an addictive organization. Michael Crosby

11

more recently has expressed similar concerns in *The Dysfunctional Church*.

Some of Peters's principles revolving around excellence were etched into my mind when I studied under him in southern California several years ago. Among them were:

1. Love your customers; without obsessive love, your customers will become someone else's customers.

2. Be innovative with your product (possible translation or implication: ... do we make the Good News boring news?).

3. As leaders divest yourselves of the trappings of power, taking on the *persona*, rather, of the coach of a team.

4. As a good coach facilitate members of the team to feel as if they are active, important members of the team's overall mission.

In his later work, *Thriving on Chaos*, Peters contends that excellence is not enough, that even since the writing of his *Excellence* books the world has radically changed. What is needed now, joined to excellence, is flexibility, a willingness on the part of an organization and its leaders to adapt constantly. Within those principles of flexibility and adaptability is a long list of admonitions for leaders to practice within organizations: listen; be extraordinarily responsive to customers; innovate models (a notion we will return to again); involve everyone in everything (in most Catholic parishes, which live out of a vertical or hierarchical ecclesiology, embraced by both clerics and laity, this will be slow in coming); simplify structures; eliminate humiliating conditions (Maslow offered this basic insight into human nature years ago); inspire vision; love change; decentralize; bash bureaucracy. These are just a few of many exciting insights.

In speaking of model innovation, Peters encourages stealing each other's ideas, that is, taking seminal thoughts and models from each other, excellent ones, and adapting them for local situations. He writes that "uniqueness most often comes not from a breakthrough idea, but from the accumulation of thousands of tiny enhancements" (*Thriving on Chaos*, 234). Model innovation amounts to creative swiping and swapping of ideas and strategies. It involves embracing apparent competitors. Model innovators congratulate and reward innovation. That is what *Parishes That Excel* is about. It takes ideas from my previous work, *Re-Imagining the Parish* — the importance of admitting organizational addiction and seeking liberation from it, of re-imagining what parish life can be like, of participating in small communities, of re-valuing adult religious education and advocating family consciousness — and shows parishes, Catholic and non-Catholic, that are putting these values into practice.

These are only models I have bumped into or read about. I offer them with pride, not to demean perhaps greater innovations on the part of communities not represented here, but to enable you, the reader, to swipe, swap, enhance, and become even more excellent in your ministry.

# CHAPTER TWO

# On Becoming a Recovering Church: Excellence in Evangelization

---

The past two years have been ones of great change in my life. I sold our family home, which we had owned since I was three years old. My father became ill and died after less than two weeks at my parents' retirement condo. My mother has recurring illnesses since the loss of her husband and home. A beloved aunt, Kate Canty, suddenly passed away. A little Yorkshire terrier, whom I named K.C. after her, died at ten months of age because of a defective heart while playing in the backyard. The middle years are often characterized by loss, and with the loss comes the shaking of some of the foundational images of our lives. In the personal situations I have spoken of above, there have been powerful directive images of *home* and *loss of home* and *finding a home within; surrendering* a loved one whom I wanted to control; reframing the *death* of an aunt (*apparent loss*) as a rediscovery of an undying *real presence;* even reframing the *loss* of a pet as an *opportunity* of having had in a little creature *a taste of God's unconditional love*.

As I have said in many parishes around the country, these past several years have been for me "breakdowns" that eventually have become "breakthroughs" to new levels of being and consciousness. The breakdown-to-breakthrough process has largely been on the level of imagination, through the help of mentoring figures and through the assistance of and celebration with communities of faith.

As individual conversion experiences are in essence a repatterning of the intrapsychic or cultural imagination with dominant images more congruent with those of Jesus, we as church are in the midst of a breakdown that hopefully will become a breakthrough. We as

14

church are in the midst of a corporate dominant image shift. Fr. Vincent Donovan reflects on this well in his book *The Church in the Midst of Creation*. He speaks of the breakdown of the Industrial Revolution parish. Get a feel, if you can, of that dominant image of church. Industrial Revolution speaks of "spiritual factory" — of centralization, mechanization, and synchronization of services, ministries, and conversion experiences. It speaks of maximization — serving, sacramentalizing large, often unevangelized numbers of people. That image of church, writes Donovan, is collapsing, giving way to a new/old image, that of the church as the instrument of a New Creation, characterized by a more human, communal tone. What is keeping us from a more felt experience of communion and community is at least in part organizational addiction: staying with what does not work, staying with life-robbing rather than life-giving strategies, and suffering loss of integrity that includes a loss of one's original vision or mission.

The mission of the church of Jesus Christ is to *evangelize*. Constitutive to breaking away from addictive ecclesiology and consequent ecclesial praxis is the need to admit the need for recovery. Addictive people and systems need to get beyond the pretense of perfection to admit the need for recovery.

A recovering church would have to admit that certain aspects of church life have become dysfunctional or unmanageable. Many of us would need to admit a certain degree of codependency or collusion with the system. We would need to trust in and turn to the Spirit of a Higher Power who can heal and help us on the road to recovery. We would need to take direct, ongoing inventory — moral and ministerial. We would need to seek *God's* will for the church. Many of those in leadership would need to seek out and make direct amends with those who have been hurt by the institutional side of the church. All of us as church would need, through daily meditation and a spiritual program, to grow in a spirit of ongoing renewal, re-evangelization, and transformation. Engaging in such a process, we would be better enabled to "get back to" our core mission, to tell the world about this healing Higher Power. Giving witness to this power in word and deed is evangelization.

A thread running through this book is a call to parishes and to all in pastoral ministry to embrace evangelization as our central mission. This will not be accomplished by the proliferation of anemic evangelization teams with little authority or power. No, a recovering church according to "the convergence model" that I wrote about in *The Evangelizing Parish* would involve all diocesan agencies, all parish boards, teams, and commissions, and all in any kind of pastoral work in any segment of the total mission of evangelization. One's gifted- ness and ministerial call would shape the nature of the involvement in the mission.

Contrary to manipulative, monological strategies of proselytizers, those in true evangelizing ministry are simply "inviting" people to a relationship of love with God in the context of community.

To evangelize necessitates pre-evangelization — an unarticulated kind of bonding in which people enter each other's world in relation- ships. In such relationships, for example with inactive Catholics, we might encounter hurt or anger. With the baptized or sacramentalized unconverted, we might confront boredom or ennui with the church or spirituality-related issues.

Pre-evangelization and evangelization lead to catechesis. The Order of Initiation has given us a whole new feeling for catechesis: According to the original Greek *katachein*, catechesis is a "re-echoing" of the primordial experiences of pre-evangelization and evangeliza- tion, that is, initial, primary conversion. Catechesis is no less than this immersion into three strata of Christian community: the large liturgical assembly, a small intentional community, and the domes- tic church of household, family, home. Certainly this is a statement of the ideal. In actuality, the *communal* or *relational* is a continuum that will be realized by individuals and communities is a variety of ways. Some people will be comfortable with "the relational" in terms of greeting another at the beginning of Mass. Others will both want and need the experience of a toe-to-toe small Christian community toward whom they have accountability.

A Mexican priest evaluating the American Catholic evangeliza- tion scene said to me that American Catholics presume that pre- evangelization and evangelization have happened because the waters of baptism have been poured. This is indeed a big presumption. From that presumption, we jump to the third step, catechesis, *re-echoing*, in effect, building on what has not happened yet and turning catechesis into a head-trip about God and church — book-learning — instead of gradual immersion into community.

Evangelization and its related ministries of pre-evangelization and catechesis are the church's central mission waiting to be rediscovered. The beneficiaries of the mission as they are referred to by Paul VI in *Evangelii Nuntiandi* (1975) are the active; the active uninvolved (often in need of re-evangelization); the baptized unconverted (or sacramentalized but unevangelized), among whom are counted many young adults; the alienated and hurt; the unchurched; children; the adolescent and young adult population; the ever-growing elderly population, now living long enough to ask profoundly deep spiritual questions that they perhaps did not feel they had permission to ask in the past; victims of systemic injustice in need of both the physical and spiritual works of mercy that are part of total evangelization; society and cultures desperately in need of spiritual transformation. These last two target areas and populations are written about brilliantly by James Fowler in *Weaving the New Creation: Stages of Faith and the Public Church.*

When a recovering church embraces its original central mission, it creates a new agenda for parishes that want to excel. Included in that agenda are:

1. *Conversion.* A parish and its ministers cannot *make* conversion happen, but we constantly need to discern whether our programs and processes are creating an environment conducive to conversion. Special attention needs to be given to the "sacramentalized, unevangelized."

2. *The evangelization of healing.* So many people distant from the Table of the Lord have Church stories cloaking other personal stories. They are in need of reconciliation with opportunities for catharsis, a ministry with opportunities for catharsis, informational update, and faith formation.

3. *The evangelization of culture and the inculturation of faith.* In their national plan for evangelization, the U.S. bishops, writing in *Go and Make Disciples: Shaping a Catholic Evangelizing People*, articulate three primary goals for American Catholic evangelization: (1) the evangelization and re-evangelization of active Catholics, (2) the evangelization of the alienated and unchurched, and (3) the evangelization of culture. This last goal is perhaps the most important yet the most elusive. George Gallup postulates that 90 percent of Americans notionally believe in God, yet that God dimension of their lives has little or no impact on their daily living or valuing. Catholics are much more American consumers than they are Christians or people of God's Reign. There is no

flashy program out there to accomplish the evangelization of
our culture, but skills for critical reflection need to be developed
that help Christians name the counter-gospel images of daily
life, evaluate them, and look to the alternatives, that is, the directive images of God's Reign. Simultaneously, as we evangelize
culture we need to inculturate faith, or allow faith to take root
in the native cultures of people. Inculturation, assimilation, integration are all activities to be kept in balance. As Allen Deck
writes, the Church in America seems to have done this well for
the first wave of immigrants to the United States, namely, Euro-
peans. But, at least numerically, we seem to be failing with the
second wave of Asians and Hispanics, as well as with African
Americans.

4. *Adult faith formation rather than a preoccupation with forming children.* Several models in the present book are examples of parishes
   trying to form adults in faith and not only children — the latter
   often done through insufficient child-oriented schooling programs. Religious educator John Westerhoff said prophetically
   years ago that our children will *not* have faith if they are not
   socialized into communities of maturing adult believers.

5. *Small intentional communities.* We will give attention less to theory and theology and more to the practice of small intentional
   communities. I insist in my teaching and lecturing on not buying into one programmatic style of small communities, but
   rather acquiring an interior discipline for participating in small
   communities: praying together, breaking open Sacred Scripture,
   sharing life, and exercising ministry — to the small group, the
   larger parish, and the market place.

6. *Family perspective.* The U.S. bishops' document *A Family Perspective in Church and Society* (1987) has challenged parishes to make
   the many styles and shapes of today's families to become lenses
   through which we do education and pastoral ministry in general. This will require a dismantling of the unnecessary walls
   erected between educational ministries and those in the social
   agencies and helping professions. A similar advocacy is found in
   the bishops' statement of November 14, 1991, *Putting Children
   and Families First: A Challenge for Our Church, Our Nation, and
   the World.*

7. *The enabling of lay leadership and lay ministry.* Though I have an antipathy for the word *lay* to describe a baptized follower of Jesus, I use it here for reasons of convenience. Just as we in pastoral leadership cannot effect conversions, so also we cannot empower people. The Spirit does the empowering. All we can do is facilitate the power and the charisms that are already there. This will involve a movement from a vertical to horizontal view of ministry, based on discernment of charisms and multiple new commissioning rites.

8. *The renewal of the clergy.* You don't have to be a wizard to sense the malaise of the clergy. A Brazilian statistic is revealing: one priest per nine thousand households. There are seven hundred priests for twenty-one hundred parishes in born-again Ukraine. As John Paul II called recently for a "new evangelization" in Brazil, some earnest bishops sadly asked "how?" — with a presbyterate restricted to celibate males. If we who remain committed to the priesthood as it is, "the last priests in America," as Tim Unsworth describes us, are to be effective, we must attend to our own ongoing renewal physically, psychologically, spiritually, and relationally. Otherwise we are little more than burned-out cases with little to offer.

9. *Collaborative ministry.* A renewed clergy will not be intimidated by truly collaborative ministry. I know priests who think they are co-laborers who are in fact only delegators. They hire people for very progressive, relevant ministries, but they fail to walk with, co-labor with their parish or volunteer ministers. Truly collaborative ministry is an ongoing process of discerning the giftedness of staffs, boards, teams, and councils, and "working with" each person as living members of the Body of Christ.

10. *Renewed ecclesiology.* As we imagine parish or church, so we "do" parish or church. The Catholic Church is still too much the church of the anonymous crowd. Such ecclesiology militates against true community and renders the latter only a jargon term. In our recovery and re-imagining we must struggle, I believe, if we are to be scripturally grounded: (a) to become a *church of disciples*, people with a close personal bond with Jesus, trying to appropriate his inner life and values; (b) a *church of Apostles*, believers who are not content with leaving Christ in

the sanctuary on Sunday, but "missioned" to bring his living presence to the marketplace; (c) a *church of stewards*, people discerning time, giftedness, and treasure for the common good and the glory of God; and (d) *a church of sympathizers:* people like Martha, Mary, Lazarus, and Zacchaeus, who brought the living Christ into their homes.

I feel the parish stories contained in this book are examples of people striving toward excellence with the new agenda created by retrieving evangelization as our central mission. I pray the agenda and the stories are not just Brennan's, but an aid toward moving back to the future to the kind of church we find in Acts 2.

# CHAPTER THREE

# Bethel Lutheran Church, Chicago's West Side: Excellence in the African American Community

---

Sometimes religious educators complain that I dichotomize or hair-split too much when I refer to the importance of *pre-evangelization*. They rightly see pre-evangelization, evangelization, and catechesis as part of a seamless garment. In part, I share that same vision. But I often use the term *pre-evangelization* because I think it accurately reflects the *process* of faith maturation. Even Paul said some folks are not ready for full spiritual food yet, but rather they are in need of something more basic — like milk. For me, pre-evangelization refers to entering the world of others and often staying there with them for a while, taking time to heal or to help them to help themselves. Some people are too broken to hear the Good News or get involved actively in parish life. In pre-evangelization, we as ministers go to people rather than demanding or expecting them to come to the parish campus. Such is the approach of Reverend David Nelson, his wife, his sister, and the rest of his staff at Bethel Lutheran Church on Chicago's West Side.

Chicago's West Garfield Park is a poor, crime-filled area, with many homes gutted or hopelessly in disrepair. The area is filled with gang warfare. The Evangelical Lutheran Church sent David Nelson there twenty-six years ago in the midst of the late 1960s urban rioting. Bethel Lutheran's German-American congregation was down to thirty-five members. One almost has to be a Chicagoan to understand the panic-peddling and urban flight, the overnight changes that occurred at the time in neighborhoods when blacks and Hispanics moved in. David Nelson and his sister Mary began their ministry with a very commonsense yet overlooked step.

Instead of emotionally and spiritually bulldozing, as many priests and pastors do upon assignment to a parish, which often among the urban poor is equivalent to plantation politics, they began an expansive *process of listening*. Notice the difference — instead of taking over a dying parish, maintaining dying programs, and eventually facing the inevitable "consolidation or closing" experience, they took on a very evangelical posture of "growing church." What was good about the past could be maintained, but more important was to leave the past (the dead, dying past) in ashes and allow God to work new life there.

The pastoral listening provided the following conclusions: first, parents felt their children needed better education than provided by what psychiatrist David Elkind calls the "schools for scandal," that is, the public school system; second, the rapidly decaying buildings, once beautiful structures, needed nurturance; third, the neighborhood's social woundedness was badly in need of healing ministry.

The Nelsons began in earnest to minister to these pre-evangelical needs. Mary Nelson, a professional educator and former missionary to Tanzania, started special tutoring programs with the assistance of hundreds of volunteers. That seminal group gave birth to Bethel New Life, a movement that established the Community Christian Alternative Academy. It has, over the years, cared for what we call the "traditional drop-out." Stephanie Jefferson, a congregation member with a master's degree and a position at the University of Illinois, has an office to help teenagers prepare for college entrance exams and to apply to colleges.

Camille Lilly, another member of the congregation, earned her master's degree in public health and now heads a division of Bethel New Life called Families with a Future. This movement has played a significant role in reducing the neighborhood's infant morality rate from 33 to 17 per 1000 children. Bethel New Life also offers, and teaches other African American churches, a variety of helping services: tutoring, meals for homeless people, and medical services that include detoxification.

To improve the housing in the neighborhood David and Mary purchased a three-room flat from the Department of Housing and Urban Development in 1978 for a mere $275. Congregation members worked together to renovate it. Bethel New Life recently worked on a ten-home townhouse development in a blighted area near the Eisenhower Expressway. This most recent effort is all part of Bethel New Life's affordable housing plan, which has helped many poor people learn how to establish credit and, for the first time in their lives, put down a small amount of money for a home of their own.

The Nelsons' work in housing has had an impact on the city of Chicago's housing plans. Not only has the mayor asked Mary Nelson to chair a committee on low-income housing but other local community groups have started "Adopt-a-Building" programs. Community social workers are trained to target a run-down housing site and motivate all those living in the building to commit themselves to a plan in which physical and spiritual needs are addressed in an ongoing way. The focus is on the spiritual uplifting of a building. Bible readings, prayer, and attendance at some church (notice Peters's notion of embracing competitors) are encouraged in addition to commitment to improving housing.

A typical Sunday church bulletin at Bethel Lutheran contains lists of job openings. Though some of the openings are for jobs "in the marketplace," many are skill-oriented and social service jobs at Bethel Lutheran or Bethel New Life Incorporated.

The white congregation of 35 some twenty-six years ago now has risen to 650 largely African American members. Individuals and families pledge an average of $20 a week, resulting in a financially self-sufficient congregation. This approach stands in marked contrast to the subsidization method of the Catholic Church. Parishes on subsidy are evangelically infantalized. Why do they need to pre-evangelize or evangelize as long as "sugar daddy/mommy" is providing funds? The problem with this approach is that, around the country, the funds have run out, and African American parishes, out of fiscal necessity, have had to go through the anguishing processes of closing or consolidation. Bethel Lutheran is an example of an alternative of experiencing church: an organic, evangelical "growing" church model vs. a top-down, centrally controlled, paternalistically subsidized model. In her book *New Life from Dying Churches,* Dr. Rose Sims maintains that Bethel-like new life can happen anywhere if only ministers better respond to "hunger and nakedness," have an attitude of love and service toward potential and actual church members, and build networks of healthy relationships among people.

In their classic study *The Black Church in the African American*

*Experience*, C. Eric Lincoln of Duke University and Lawrence H. Mamiya of Vassar examine the health of African American churches in the United States. They study the seven largest black Protestant denominations in the country: the National Baptist Convention, USA, Inc.; the National Baptist Convention of America; the Progressive National Baptist Convention, Inc.; the African Methodist Episcopal Church (A.M.E.); the African Methodist Episcopal Zion Church; the Christian Methodist Episcopal Church; and the Church of God in Christ. The two scholars found that the congregations with more traditional modes of operation and expression in worship attract many senior citizens. But the congregations that offer Spirit-filled worship, an experience of Jesus of great immediacy, and the opportunity for spiritual rebirth — joined to efforts to remedy economic and social ills — are the ones that seem to attract the greatest numbers, across the widest age span. They also point out that Islam is attracting many young black men because of its emphasis on male assertiveness, black pride, and discipline. Lincoln and Mamiya believe that some form of Pentecostalism will claim the allegiance of half of black churchgoers before this century is over. Studying Lincoln and Mamiya, one gets the impression that flourishing black congregations offer people both spiritual and *social* hope.

What we have talked about thus far is well summarized by Kennan L. Callahan in his book *Effective Church Leadership*. He describes the task of a pastor:

> The church is...not...an end to itself; [it exists] to help persons discover fulfillment in their search for individuality, community, meaning, and hope.... The central leadership task for the missionary pastor is to help persons to discover some sense of hope.... This is not best done by drawing people into a "ghetto where God lives." In that case, the church would be creating its own compartmentalization — alienation and fragmentation — dehumanization. God calls us not to live apart from the world but to live in the world.... The art is to identify...specific hurt and...deliver concrete, effective help.... One thus attacks the human hurt in a wholistic way. (135–36)

Callahan contends that churches can no longer afford to stress the professional minister vs. laity dichotomy. All people in a congregation have to come to experience themselves as God's missionaries. He contends that while traditional churches stress functions, a conservative holding-on, the church campus, church programs, institutional leadership, and professional ministers, successful churches focus on the relational aspects of life, take risks with their resources, look to the real world instead of church property, foster life searches instead of programs, support an externally focused leadership, and see both clergy and laity as "God's missionaries." The days of a focus on professional ministry are over, he says. The focus now must be on *mission*. A parish or church is either about mission or about institutional maintenance.

# CHAPTER FOUR

# St. Michael's Catholic Church, Milwaukee: Excellence in Multicultural Ministry

In many of my recent talks and lectures, taking note of the Hispanic, Asian, European and other racial-ethnic immigration patterns, I encourage my listeners to invest in becoming students of culture. One of the most enjoyable aspects of my ministry as the director of the Office for Evangelization in Chicago is to meet with Asian, African American, Hispanic, and European consultants to the archdiocese's agencies. I never leave a meeting without having learned something from them. At a recent meeting, they shared with me and my co-director, Dawn Mayer Melendez, that the Catholic Church can rest secure with first-generation Hispanic immigrants. They remain loyal. But second- and third-generation Hispanic immigrants are not so loyal, and, because of poor inculturation and evangelization have either switched allegiance to evangelical groups or are "going nowhere," that is, have become functionally unchurched. The Asian and European consultants confided that they are convinced the church is losing *first*-generation immigrants to this country. At the turn of the twentieth century and in the two or three decades following it, European immigrants were the backbone and builders of the church. They left us many of the edifices we now have — which unfortunately have become financial burdens and aesthetic blights — in our large urban centers. The current first-generation immigrants are uncomfortable with a poorly explained post–Vatican II American church, devoid of devotion, especially to Mary. These recent

26

immigrants gravitate to crowded parishes that "seem to understand them." In effect, they cross the traditional canonical boundary lines to go to a parish that appears to be a "home." Others "find a priest" who offers Eucharist or devotions at a center or in someone's home. Some become functionally unchurched though devotionally Catholic.

Many American parishes of the future, not just in the city, but also in the suburbs and rural areas, will be multicultural parishes. The goal, I believe, in such parishes will be to enable unique cultural groups to experience and celebrate faith in their own native culture, while also meeting, merging, and celebrating with other cultural expressions. St. Michael's parish in Milwaukee is attempting to accomplish such a goal. The style that I observe at St. Michael's is one of *progress*, not perfection, that is, the staff slowly tries to learn and shape rather than presume that in such a culturally diverse milieu as theirs they will do everything perfectly.

St. Michael's is a multicultural parish of fourteen hundred people in the city of Milwaukee. The pastor is Father Richard Broach, a wise, humble, brash, adventurous, forty-ish priest. The demographics of the parish break down somewhat like this. About four hundred are Hmong. The Hmong are from the highlands of Laos. Historically influenced by the Chinese, their native spirituality is a hybrid of animism and Buddhism. They did not have any written language until fifty-five years ago.

St. Michael's also has about four hundred Hispanics. Anyone who has been exposed to multicultural ministry knows that *Hispanic* is a tent-like term housing many subpopulations. Specifically, at St. Michael's most Hispanics are either Mexican or Puerto Rican.

There are about two hundred Caucasians of various ethnic roots and about fifty African Americans. Some three hundred others from various parts of the metropolitan area have found St. Michael's to be home, a fascinating place to be.

Dick Broach ministers on the basis of three principles regarding culture:

1. *enculturation:* This term, Broach suggests, refers to how we have all grown up in our homes and families.

2. *inculturation:* This refers to the process in which the message of Christianity permeates a culture.

3. *acculturation:* This refers to two or more cultures mixing and interacting with one other. Ideally, such cultures mingle with one other in a natural process over time. The danger of acculturation is that mutual mingling, at least in part, has led to the domination of one culture over another. The domination, in turn, has led to the assimilation and consequent evaporation of the culture of lesser power, popularly known as colonialization.

In terms of pastoral strategy, Broach and his staff have four guiding principles. They call them the *four Is:*

1. The integrity of each culture in the parish is to be reverenced and respected.

2. The gospel must be inculturated. When the gospel is taken into a new culture, something radically new emerges. In this process, evangelizers and ministers are simultaneously transformed, as are the evangelized. This is a true experience of *incarnation*, or the Word taking flesh in a culture. The presence of God already in a culture emerges. This is the opposite of insisting that a culture conform to a given expression of the gospel, often resulting in domination and assimilation.

3. The various cultures within the parish need to *interact*.

4. Newly arriving immigrant cultures need some degree of integration into American culture, though there is a danger because the dominant American culture is consumerism.

The above principles, Broach says, were arrived through, prayer, reflection, listening to the people, reading church documents and other research, and the previous experience in multicultural ministry of staff members. Though the acronym might scandalize some, the staff's modus operandi is: ascertain your direction; sally forth; see what happens (A.S.S.).

One of three Hmong deacons in the United States is at St. Michael's. This reflects Broach's conviction that as much as possible indigenous leadership should be provided the various subcultures. He makes a distinction between pastoral and ordained leadership, placing the former on a footing equal to that of the ordained. Of the 1400 members of the parish, 30 percent are under the age of twelve. Approximately 350 are in the children's faith formation program.

The St. Michael's staff strives for the representation and participation of all cultures. This is attempted in the bulletin, in parish governance (parish council), in staffing, and in the standing committees of the parish. Part of the parish's genius is that each culture has its own governing board. Parish council decisions and communications from the staff are filtered through these subgoverning boards.

Music is another important symbol for cultural representation. The parish hymnal contains songs in four different languages. People are encouraged to sing each other's music. Music is a way for cultures to learn from and about each other. Not just unique cultural expression but integration is thus promoted.

There is an interplay between inculturation and acculturation, between a healthy separatism and an equally healthy integration. Ministers with a great need for neatness and programmatic efficiency might experience a lot of anxiety at St. Michael's. The 4:30 Saturday afternoon Mass of anticipation is in English. The 9:00 A.M. Sunday Mass is trilingual. The noon Mass is both in Spanish and English. But sometimes during the year the schedule is collapsed to bring all cultures together. At some liturgies, incense sticks are used to appeal to former Buddhists and their animistic worldview. Similarly Order of Initiation rituals are adapted for the various cultures: a string around the wrists for a Laotian is equivalent to signing one with the cross, that is, calling a candidate for initiation to commitment and self-sacrificial love.

This multicultural, synergistic parish is not without its problems. Simultaneous translation at meetings, which is held as a parish value, is sometimes difficult to provide and tedious to experience. In terms of pastoral-ecclesial formation and training, people coming from an animistic or Buddhist background have roots almost antithetical to American pragmatism. The bridging of the two totally different worldviews is quite difficult. Hispanics are often still clergy-bound, overly respectfully of the clergy and personally nonresponsive, waiting for the clergy "to do" for them. Among Hispanics there can also be multileveled subcultures — each with its own nuance of language and customs. (e.g., Puerto Rican, Mexican, Peruvian, etc.). Among Hispanic subgroups there is a reluctance to be both a reflection of one's own subculture while simultaneously a bridge to others in the parish. As with most parishes today, finances are problematic. St. Michael's raises approximately one-third of its budget through parishioners' contributions, relying on bingo, fund-raising projects, grants, and archdiocesan subsidy for the rest.

I was impressed by St. Michael's processes for faith formation. In establishing its current approach to religious education, the staff asked the people and families involved what kind of format would help and please them. The convergence of opinion was anchored in the Sunday morning experience and liturgy. Families gather once a month on the first Sunday, between the 9:00 am and noon liturgies, so people are free to attend whichever liturgy most appeals to them. At these gatherings, adults separate for adult catechesis, and children for children's catechesis. Families with children in grade three through high school gather in same-language adults' and children's groups. Groups of children in kindergarten through grade two are bilingual — Spanish and English. One theme is covered each month. The children return to their parents toward the end of the session for a family religious experience. The session ends with each subgroup or culture learning key words and symbols from other cultures. Between monthly sessions, hand-outs provide an opportunity for continued faith formation in the home. Children by themselves cannot become part of this process. Only families, whether two-parent, single parent, blended, or supervised by some guardian, can participate. Adult involvement is mandatory. It takes about forty trained ministers to implement this catechetical effort. Someone becomes a minister by apprenticing in the process for an appropriate period. The process is both informational and formational.

The Sunday process is supplemented with other efforts. On a regular basis there is children's Liturgy of the Word. The children are dismissed for their own service of the Word and process back in to be with the adults at the presentation of gifts. Children are trained also to be "players" who mime or dramatize Scripture. There are culturally respectful processions for sacramental moments. The catechumenate at St. Michael's includes separate, culturally sensitive gatherings. The rites are performed together, however, and the sponsors are cross-cultural. Small Christian communities are fostered and encouraged. The natural weavings, the occasion for people to gather are many: the aging, baby-boomers, Hispanics, Charismatics, Bible study groups, Laotians, youth, and other natural groupings. Broach admits that Caucasians still tend to assume leadership more readily than others.

Human life and social concerns are important at St. Michael's. Socializing is promoted. Celebrations of various kinds are offered

# MISSION STATEMENT FOR ST. MICHAEL'S

The St. Michael's Faith Community is a unique reflection of the universality of the Catholic Church and as such shares the joys and challenges that such diversity brings:

**We celebrate**
the diversity of peoples, languages, cultures, and ways of thinking we represent.

**We are challenged by**
the struggles to maintain and strengthen Christian unity in the midst of such diversity while not losing the uniqueness of the individual person or culture.

**We celebrate**
the opportunity to witness the gospel to the poor and marginalized of Milwaukee's Central City.

**We are challenged by**
the struggle to meet physical and spiritual needs with limited resources.

**We celebrate**
our continuing tradition of being a place of refuge especially for immigrant peoples.

**We are challenged by**
the need to find creative and effective ways of communicating the Word of God.

**We celebrate**
our Patron, St. Michael, defender of truth.

**We are challenged by**
the call to grow in faith and to more effectively live the gospel call to be People of Justice.

**We celebrate**
our faith heritage and tradition of hospitality and outreach.

**We are challenged and commit ourselves to**
reach out to the people in our neighborhood through evangelization and education and to find ways to help the youth of our community to build on their heritage as they move the church into the future.

**We celebrate especially the Eucharist**
for it is here that we find our unity and our strength and hope for the future.

throughout the year. There are common celebrations, but each culture is also encouraged to have its own. The staff try to help integrate the cultures by getting the people involved in "hands-on" projects — like decorating the church. In fact, the church was recently completely renovated by the people. Broach says that this renovation was an important symbolic act, emphasizing that the parish church is the *people's* church, not the staff's. The convent has been converted into temporary housing for refugees. Parishioners have worked with and been trained by the police in the prevention of crime and violence. St. Michael's staff have served as advocates to the police department and have requested full-time translators for the department.

One of Richard Broach's guiding principles for himself and his staff is: Watch out for fatigue and frustration. He prays for an enduring belief in the *power of God* working in the parish and subcommunities. Proselytizers from evangelical groups are not a threat to him. If they benefit people, let people go to them. He can only do what he can do. He practices "letting go" and "letting them (the people of God) do." "I don't have to be everything," he says, "yet I pray for and work at staying motivated for this very worthwhile work." There is a kind of staff mutual monitoring system. Each staff member must take one day off a week, as well as additional "sanity" days when needed. No one can work more than eight or nine hours per day. These therapeutic measures are taken to avoid burn-out and to insure an upbeat staff of ministers.

Five years ago when St. Michael's was in the midst of much demographic change, only the basement needed to be used for the worship of a dwindling congregation. Now the church has been renovated and there is a need to add seating — a healthy problem and the sign of a lot of excellent and innovative work.

# CHAPTER FIVE

# Willowcreek Community Church, South Barrington, Ill.: Excellence in the Church Growth Movement and Reach-Out to the Unchurched

---

My first assignment as an ordained minister was next door to Willowcreek Community Church, which hold its services in the now shuttered Willowcreek cinema, a typical sterile suburban movie theater. As I think back, the Willowcreek movement has long been a thorn in my side — or a challenge to learn and grow. In 1972, as I served as a deacon at St. Paul of the Cross parish in Park Ridge, Illinois, with a responsibility to minister to youth. I was aware that a couple of young ministers were attracting lots of Catholic, Protestant, and unchurched young people in a youth movement called Son City, housed in a nearby Protestant church and coordinated by a young man named Bill Hybels. I moved to Hoffman Estates, Illinois, in 1973; Hybels moved to contiguous Palatine and the Willowcreek Theater in 1975.

Hybels replicated, even improved, his successful Son City for youth in these far northwestern suburbs of Chicago. But he also tried to build on the youth movement and to develop the congregation for people of all ages. Specifically, he wanted to create a church for the unchurched, for those whom he calls in his talks "the unchurched Harrys." He targeted the many people, especially the young adults, married and single, who either had ceased active practice in their church of origin or had never had a faith home. The original team that moved with Hybels from Park Ridge to Palatine began some nonproselytizing home visitation to discern what kind of church the unchurched might feel attracted to. The listening sessions confirmed a conviction that Hybels, of Christian Reformed roots, held from his youth: that organized religions had packaged Jesus in such a way that he had become boring and irrelevant. Most of those interviewed said that they did not go to church because it was boring. Hybels had decided early on in his ministry that he would not contribute to the sterilization of the power and image of Jesus.

Hybels's meager beginnings and brilliant "evangelization as marketing" strategies have led in sixteen years to 15,000 weekly worshippers; a $15 million building, opened in 1981; a projected $18 million, 200,000-square-foot addition with a ministry center, classrooms, and basketball courts (we will see the power of basketball courts shortly); a weekly collection of $175,000; a staff of 250; a $9-million budget; ninety ministries — most of them very practical and down-to-earth; and at least 250 small Christian communities with about 2500 members. (A ten-week series of sermons on twelve-step spirituality recently raised the congregation to 18,000 weekly.) Hybels laments that there are not more small communities, but to take on a commitment to a small community involves a third night or day of involvement for the committed Willowcreek member. Perhaps such time demands are unrealistic. Nonetheless, Hybels remains undaunted in his commitment to small groups, because that is how Jesus worked and discipled. For Hybels, small groups are not a "should we?" question, but a "how?" question.

One of the primary mentors in Bill Hybels's life was Gilbert Bilezikian, a Scripture professor at Wheaton college. Bilezikian confirmed Hybels's intuition that mainline churches did not appeal to many people of the television age. In *Re-imagining the Parish*, I contended that the Roman Catholic Church was organizationally addicted to medieval, traditionalist (not even traditional) ways of being and doing church. Hybels and Bilezikian contend that mainline Protestantism has been and is in similar shape, rooted in attitudes and practices from the sixteenth century and the Reformation era.

I asked Bill Hybels to address a Roman Catholic group in the archdiocese of Chicago recently. Sadly, only a handful showed up, and two clerics walked out in the middle of his presentation because they found him "too evangelical." Evangelical and fundamentalistic he is.

But he is gentle, sincere — and obviously touching some very real needs. Estimates of the number of former Roman Catholics attending Willowcreek range from 50 to 80 percent. To cover my brother priests' rudeness and to get to the point, I asked a question.

"Bill, why are you attracting so many Catholics?"

Hybels looked down at his feet, carefully collecting his thoughts before he spoke. Then he said, "Too many of your parishes are on auto-pilot. You basically just offer your Eucharist as the standard bill of fare. I respect your Eucharist, but, especially for many young adults, it is too much, too rich. In addition, I think many baptized Catholics and Protestants are not convinced Christians. Expecting young adults to enjoy or get something out of your Mass is like dropping one of us into the middle of a Moslem service. It would be totally foreign to us."

Hybels went on to explain his church's strategies. The Sunday morning experience is known as a seeker service. It is presumed that the vast majority of attendees are "unconvicted," that is, not converted. Contemporary Christian rock and softer Christian ballads replace traditional hymns. Frequently contemporary morality plays augment the day's message. Hybels and others who preach at the service focus their messages on practical aspects of daily living: marriage, parenting, finances, work, improving relationships. Scripture quotes pepper the preaching, and participants are encouraged to turn to each passage and read along. "Unchurched Harry" can maintain anonymity as long as he (or she) wants to. But each Sunday service closes with two admonitions: (1) to come out of anonymity and become a more active member of the church by dropping your name in one of the baskets at the exits of the church, and (2) to reach out in a spirit of mission and bring someone to church the following week. When people drop their names in the baskets, the affinity ministry team calls them before Monday evening, encouraging them to get involved in membership classes, a small group, or the Wednesday/Thursday evening sessions.

The 7:30 P.M. Wednesday/Thursday gathering is the equivalent of catechesis in Catholic culture. The crowd of seekers is much smaller at these gatherings than on Sunday — perhaps several hundred each evening. Scripture study is combined with a series on a topic of interest. For example, a recent series was entitled "Turning Points." It was about adult life-change and conversion experiences. The entire series was scripturally based. A four-point outline was distributed with four key insights. Ample room was provided for people to take notes. On occasion there is a celebration of the Lord's Supper. The distinction between Sunday seeker services and the Wednesday/Thursday sessions for the convicted is an example of the importance that Willowcreek places on discernible conversion.

Each week's bulletin contains news of the over ninety ministries. A page is also given to the welcoming of new members, with a sentence or two describing each new member. Space is given to mention people in need of prayer and their problems and concerns. Self-help groups and their meeting times are printed regularly. Employment opportunities at the church are regularly announced. A weekly update is given on the budget — on both the needs and the responsible use of the people's donations. Special counseling and pastoral care ministries are explained. The bulletin is a tool of both information and networking.

Willowcreek began as a young people's church. It is currently undergoing remarkable demographic change. Middle-aged and elderly people are now leaving their churches of origin or their status as "unchurched" to become part of the fifteen hundred worshippers. The Sunday experience is no easy task. Special sensitivity is given in the parking lot — to the handicapped, but also the elderly and single parents, who have to contend with dangerous walks through the lot with their small children.

I regularly invite Willowcreek personnel to be resources for the archdiocesan ministers — on anything from youth evangelization to small groups to pastoring. This cross-denominational interaction extends beyond Willowcreek and Catholic parishes. Many from mainline Protestant parishes also seek Hybels's counsel. As Catholics, we learn from Willowcreek about people skills. They are genuinely hospitable in a nonmanipulative way. Willowcreek personnel have travelled to France and Spain to offer training in regenerating churches. Now other churches, like Christ Church in Oakbrook, Stone Baptist Church in Palos Heights, and the Midwest Christian Life Center in Tinley Park, all in Illinois, model their structures and series on Willowcreek vision and strategies. Willowcreek has recently purchased land in Libertyville, Illinois, to start a second Willowcreek-type church.

———

Willowcreek seems to reflect an emerging pattern in American religious life: the mega- or superchurch. First Baptist in Hammond, Indiana, is reported to be the largest in the country, with 20,000 in attendance. This is followed by Willowcreek with 15,000. Calvary Chapel in Santa Ana, California, claims 12,000 worshippers. Second Baptist in Houston has 11,500 in regular attendance. Thomas Road Baptist Church in Lynchburg, Virginia, has 11,000, and the First Assembly of God in Phoenix has 10,000.

The megachurches attract two thousand or more worshippers each weekend. Spiritual experiences are often offered hand in hand with entertainment and social activities. They appeal to the video generation, often using marketing techniques, like billboards, that traditional churches might find inappropriate. Like Willowcreek, Second Baptist in Houston does not have a traditional cross and steeple. Clear glass and nature put the worshipper in contact with the transcendent. Second Baptist even has two restaurants, appealing to different diets. A glass aerobics center begins workouts at 6:00 A.M. Rev. H. Edwin Young, who originally had been called to start a small, mainline-style congregation, had a great sensitivity to the demographics of the area: more and more singles and young families were moving to his part of the Houston area. Some grassroots research also revealed that most were unchurched. In a relatively short time, Young and his growing young congregation put up $34 million complex. He also commissioned teams of parishioners to go out to study corporate success stories — Xerox, IBM, Disney World — all in an effort to do what Peters calls model innovation or idea swapping. He is trying to borrow from the corporate world what works with "real people."

At Second Baptist, David Hutton, a former oil-field worker, is in charge of parking lot efficiency, operating with the philosophy that the customer is always right. A recent Young sermon series was entitled "How to Make Your Marriage Sizzle." The series attracted many who sat and took notes. "P.M. Houston" is the title of the Sunday evening series designed to attract young adults, with guitar music and Christian rock. Lighting and environment are adjusted to attract senior citizens to the "Ripple Creek Gathering" on Wednesday night. In a separate chapel on Wednesday nights, Christian hard rock is heard at the "Solid Rock" experiences, which attract hundreds of adolescents.

The motivation of those who come to America's contemporary megachurches varies. Some come looking for companionship or a future spouse. Others come with a deep spiritual hunger and the need for contemporary packaging. The motivation of Hybels and Young seems to be deeply spiritual, to translate the gospel for today's society.

There are various criticisms of the megachurches. Some say the megacrowds prevent fellowship and intimacy. Paul Tillich warned against churches that lack depth. Others criticize the megachurches as not involved in works of social justice. Yet both Willowcreek and Second Baptist are making more and more attempts at communal works of mercy.

Second Baptist received some criticism recently when it joined worship to wrestling matches. Yet Young, Hybels, and others con-. tend that no organization will grow if it does not actively engage in *marketing*. What is marketing? My fellow students at a Tom Peters's seminar taught me the essentials: "Marketing is helping people discover needs that they do not even know they have yet, then offering your product as a help or an answer." Another commented: "Marketing is transforming boredom, disinterest, ennui, or even anger into curiosity, interest, want, need, buying — in our case, Christ and community." The Peters seminar convinced me of the interconnectedness between marketing and what we understand as evangelization.

———

Besides the paradigmatic megachurches we have already highlighted, other "marketing" churches are making their influence felt. All Saints Episcopal Church, in Pasadena, California, has adopted a *needs-based* approach to evangelization and faith formation, ministering to both families in need of child care assistance and those suffering with AIDS. Metropolitan African American Methodist Episcopal Church in Washington, D.C., employs a variety of spiritual disciplines in specifically reaching out to African Americans. Lincoln Square Synagogue on Manhattan's Upper West Side targets Jewish intellectuals and young adults, transforming its congregations into people with a mission consciousness regarding the social ills surrounding them. Riverbed Baptist Church in Alixin, Texas, regularly uses the telephone to ask nearby residents what they need from a church and what kind of church they would attend. We will explore later a Catholic congregation that has employed similar telephone evangelization efforts. Rev. Gerald Mann from Riverbed complements his telephone and congregational efforts with television broadcasts. Here also the preaching and teaching are pragmatic applications of gospel principles to daily living.

"Marketing" churches also have their critics. Yet most of the congregations that we have highlighted contend that they indeed preach "tough discipleship," that is, a conservative Christian lifestyle, although they have begun to realize this can be done only through the lens of contemporary culture.

These spiritual entrepreneurs have made me wonder. As I see on the evening news Catholic bishops, gathered in synod, wearing headdress and garb from medieval times, I wonder if these modern-day "marketers" of the message have an insight, an approach that we — mainline Protestants and Roman Catholics — need at least to study, To respond to revelation, after all, is not to harken back to a God of the past but rather to experience a God speaking in the present moment. Ministry and parishes ought to create environments in which the *God of the present* can be heard and experienced.

At a recent gathering a young Roman Catholic priest was uncomfortable with my suggestion that we have something to learn from the Willowcreekers of the world. He especially took exception to the churches with restaurants, work-out groups, and basketball courts as part of their complexes. But Robert Whitt, a former University of Kentucky basketball player and a professed agnostic, went to Houston's Second Baptist at his girlfriend's invitation. His motivation was to please her and get into a few good basketball games. He is now a born-again Christian, converted by the integrity of gospel living he saw in the men with whom he played basketball.

God works in mysterious ways. As ministers and leaders we need to discern whether our adherence to "tradition" and "traditional" ways of doing church is getting obstructing God's mysterious ways.

# CHAPTER SIX

# St. James in Arlington Heights, Ill.: Excellence in Small Christian Communities

---

The Spirit seems to be moving "back to the future" toward the elements of the church at its birth, as documented in the second chapter of the Acts of the Apostles in the story of Pentecost. Those key pieces are:

- a sensitivity to and cooperation with the movement of the Holy Spirit

- clear and explicit evangelization about the impact that Jesus can have on life (as described by Peter)

- the transformation of anonymous crowds into spiritual seekers ("what should we do?" asked Peter's listeners)

- the reconnection of sacramental rituals with real-life conversion ("change your lives, and be baptized," was Peter's reply)

- the experience of community on at least three levels: large church, small intentional community, domestic church of family

- the ministry of the entire community based on needs and charisms

- a living out of baptismal spirituality

- a real sense of mission, both in terms of tending to real-life needs and proclaiming the message to the marketplace.

The approach that we have taken in the archdiocese of Chicago to encourage small communities has been to try to imbue in parish leaders an interior discipline regarding how to do small communities. Our staff says that almost any catechetical or formational material can be used, once the interior discipline is appropriated. Some parishes have turned to prepackaged programs materials like RENEW or the Little Rock Scripture Study. Others have decided to "grow their own" after working with Father Art Baranowski of the archdiocese of Detroit, Rosemary Blueher of the diocese of Joliet, and me. These organic growth models are among the most exciting for me, for they display the use of pastoral imagination. St. James Catholic Church in Arlington Heights, Illinois, and St. Michael's Catholic parish in Orland Park have gone the farthest in small community development. However, all the parishes in the archdiocese with a commitment to small communities, approximately twenty, have begun a peer-to-peer mentoring process to support and challenge each other. We will return to the notion of such pastoral alliances later.

Before analyzing the fine work being done at St. James we will articulate some foundational principles about small communities.

1. In a fragmented society like American culture, where independence and isolation are emphasized, small communities appeal to some who are searching for meaning and healing.

2. Small communities are not new programs or pastoral Band Aids for the clergy shortage. Rather "home churches" have both Jewish and Greek sociological roots. They are how church was experienced in its first centuries.

3. To begin small communities requires that potential members do precontracting and contracting. Precontracting involves a seminal small group in effect saying "How about . . . ?" to each other, then approaching others with the idea. Contracting more formally gets to the goals, ideals, and practicalities of when and how the community will meet.

4. Communities gradually generate a sacred *bond*, which keeps members aligned with each other.

5. Communities go through stages, as do ordinary relationships. The leaders of small communities engage in ongoing evaluation with the group asking, "Who are we? How are we doing? Where are we going?"

6. Leadership training is necessary for effective groups. This training is both a prologue to starting a group and a staple for ongoing formation.

7. Small communities require multiple ministries. At all costs, small communities want to avoid a new form of clericalism wherein only one person ministers to the others.

8. Ministry within a small community requires a discernment of charisms. Charisms refer to a person's unique share in the power of the Holy Spirit, used not for self-aggrandizement, but rather for the common good and the glory of God. Discernment comes from the Latin *discernere*, to sort out. In a small community of multiple ministries, discernment of who is gifted for each ministry replaces volunteering for tasks.

9. Small communities need to remain connected to the larger parish. Contiguity prevents small communities from degenerating into maintenance-minded cliques rather than focusing on their true purpose: mission and evangelization.

10. Small communities have four main ingredients, according to Michael Cowan and Bernard Lee in *Dangerous Memories:* (a) shared prayer; (b) shared Scripture; (c) shared life stories; (d) ministry, within the group, to the parish, to the world.

11. A natural weaving or healthy self-interest brings people together in small communities. Small communities cannot be imposed from on high by a pastor, a DRE, or another staff member. Some natural connections include extended families, neighbors, those with common life experiences, those in common ministries, those who favor seasonal gatherings (e.g., fall and Lent).

12. Communities avoid falling into a maintenance mode by reaching out for new members. The symbol of an empty chair can serve as a reminder to the group of its need to reach out and evangelize.

13. Small communities could begin *now* if people in volunteer ministry engaged in the four steps of community living described in point 10 above.

14. A core learning group focussed on small communities often is a good beginning for a parish. This core learning group then

becomes a teaching and consulting resource for the staff and parish council.

15. Community leaders need to be sensitive: everyone has a "threshold of self-disclosure" that needs to be respected in a group.

16. Similarity in church involvement attracts. The "very involved" rarely influence the marginally involved. Like attract like.

17. To renew a parish, small communities need the support of the pastor and the staff. Otherwise small communities nurture only a few. To be an instrument of parochial transformation, the staff's engagement and support are crucial.

18. Small communities change and need shaping with the passage of time. When their original contract has been accomplished, some communities die. The group should not just walk away from each other, but rather grieve and do appropriate closure.

19. Ideally, small communities do not engage only in self-nurturance, but also in politicization, that is, putting into action the values and directive images of the Reign of God.

20. Small communities require patient, diligent attention and ministry. Opposing forces are at work in Western culture: some people will aggressively seek to belong to a small community; many will seek to flee from it with equal energy.

———

St. James began to explore small Christian communities in 1989–90. During that period, Father Art Baranowski, along with me, travelled the archdiocese, sharing a new vision of church, one not rooted in programs and volunteer ministries, but in an ecclesiology and praxis of community. St. James became part of the peer-to-peer parish alliance that supported each other in the following months. St. James is a middle-class, upper-middle-class, and, in some cases, upper-class community in the northwest suburbs of Chicago. It is a very well staffed parish, known for its progressive vision and style.

While studying various components of small communities, the parish also decided to do a parish need discernment. Adult formation and spiritual renewal was constantly reiterated as the most significant need in the parish. The first step toward small communities was to try more consciously to instill in already existing groups, programs, and ministries some communal dimension, for example, prayer, or life and faith sharing. It was in effect to make parish volunteerism less "tasky." As this was being done, a committee began to put together a proposal to introduce small faith-sharing groups to the entire congregation in the spring of 1991.

The Small Christian Community Core Team was formed:

1. to identify formats and processes to offer in the spring of 1991;

2. to review and evaluate each such program;

3. from the various possibilities, to offer parishioners options and alternatives for involvement;

4. and finally, to choose several of the options and present the proposal.

Eighteen program formats were evaluated by the core team:

1. Renew

2. Genesis 2

3. Pathways

4. Parish Renewal Weekends (Chuck Gallagher Model)

5. the mission version of Parish Renewal Weekends

6. Christ Renews His Parish

7. Life in the Spirit Seminars

8. Neighborhood Mission (a small-group mission in a home, followed by small community development)

9. adaptations of the Order of Initiation

10. Romans 8

11. Sheed and Ward booklets

12. Fully Alive (John Powell)

13. Post Renew Parish Spirituality (a process that I have developed)

14. Little Rock Scripture Study

15. The Home Church

16. Creating Small Faith Communities (Fr. Art Baranowski)

17. Celebrating Life Retreat

18. Various Serendipity materials (Lyman Coleman, author)

The eighteen possibilities were narrowed to ten. Two modes were eventually offered, but a lot of work was needed before that point could be reached.

It was decided that several tools would be used in launching this small community movement. A four-night Lenten mission would be preached on "new ways of being church" as we approach the twenty-first century. Before the mission, the pastor, Peter Bowman, would speak on a renewed ecclesiology and the history of and present need for small communities. Sign-up for small communities would take place on the last night of the mission and on the weekend following the mission. The core team engaged in this strategy after consultation with the staff and the parish council. Five committees were formed by the core team: a group for ongoing study of styles of small groups, a mission committee, a publicity committee, a recruitment committee, and a prayer network for the intention of the success of the whole effort. Chairpersons were appointed for each committee. They were to:

1. establish an overall implementation approach for their segment of the project;

2. identify tasks and time lines for the subcommittee;

3. determine resource needs;

4. begin recruitment for the subcommittee.

For a successful launching of the Lenten mission and small groups, the subcommittee began work around Labor Day 1990.

After study of the eighteen possible programs, it was decided that small communities would be offered in two styles or formats. "Issues" is a series that focuses on theological or spiritual topics and topics related to daily living. Materials were gathered by the staff, the group leaders, and the director of the process, Deacon Armand Ferrini, based on ongoing discernment of needs and interests. While the materials would vary from series to series (in other words, the material is very eclectic), group leaders were trained in the basic skills of small group facilitators. The second format is entitled "Scripture Series: The Word." Although "Issues" also includes Scripture, "The Word" focuses on the following Sunday's lectionary readings. Discussion questions were put together by Deacon Ferrini and the group leaders involved in "The Word."

In preparation for the Lenten 1991 mission and small groups, a brochure was distributed to all parishioners, with questions and answers about the St. James small communities movement, now officially called "Connected." The questions and answers were designed to market "Connected." Below are the questions that Ferrini and his committee came up with.

**You probably have a few questions about "Connected"...**

**Q. I'm already in some programs at St. James.**
A. That's great. Stay in there. We want them to continue flourishing. "Connected" is an experience of spiritual application to our lives by focusing on spiritual issues and discussing those issues with the people we especially care about. If you are in a Scripture-based group or discussion/action group, you may already be satisfied.

**Q. What is my commitment to the small group?**
A. The first phase lasts about seven weeks. You and/or your group can decide the next step.

**Q. What does it cost?**
A. The materials cost less than $5.00 per person.

**Q. Who leads the group?**
A. Each group will have a trained discussion leader. He or she helps guide the meeting and gets appropriate material to assist the group to share and learn together.

**Q. What do the facilitators do?**
A. They are trained to help participants gain the maximum benefit from the subject being discussed.

**Q. How do we sign up?**
A. During the Mission Week (February 18–21) registration cards will be provided at the Mission or at Mass the following weekend, or you can call the parish office.

## Q. How will the groups be formed?

A. Three ways: (1) If a group of 10–15 who have been together at the mission decide they want to stay together, then they are a group; (2) individuals can register and they will be matched with the type of group they choose to be in; (3) individuals can join with others and form their own group.

## Q. How often do we meet?

A. We anticipate that the group will meet weekly for the first seven sessions to finish the first phase by April 1. Each group can set its own schedule after the first phase.

## Q. Is it like the "Christ Renews His Parish" program?

A. Yes and no.

No, there is no weekend experience or putting on a program for the next group.

Yes, we hope to recapture and retain a warm and spiritual feeling of oneness with God, of being nurtured in friendship and caring for others in our group.

## Q. What if I like the small Christian community experience, but am uncomfortable with the group?

A. Discuss it with your facilitator. He or she will help make the necessary arrangements to get you into a group that more closely meets your expectations.

## Q. How do these small Christian communities "connect" with each other?

A. Through the regular meetings of facilitators. These meetings will also help the facilitators to identify needed learning tools, to clarify any subjects, and to determine how well the groups are "connecting" with the topics.

## Q. Do they meet and just pray?

A. No. There is prayer, but it is not the whole meeting. The small Christian community experience deals with life issues and Scripture.

## Q. How are the facilitators chosen?

A. They are persons with past experience as group leaders or with a desire to be a facilitator. There will be initial and ongoing training to help each facilitator become more comfortable and more effective with a group.

## "CONNECTED" PROFILE
### August 1991

|  | no. of groups | no. of participants |
|---|---|---|
| "Connected" groups | 23 | 242 |
| Miscellaneous groups affiliated with "Connected" | 12 | 161 |
| Women's CRHP Groups | 3 | |
| Marriage Encounter Groups | 3 | |
| Spread Facilitators | 1 | |
| RCIA | 1 | |
| Neighborhood Groups | 4 | |
| Little Rock Groups | 11 | 84 |
| Quest Groups | 25 | 402 |
| **Total Small Faith Communities** | **71** | **889** |

**Q.  Do I have to tell everybody about my life?**
A.  Absolutely not. You are free to speak as much or as little as you wish. This is a learning, caring experience, not a talking experience.

**Q.  Can I join both groups?**
A.  Yes. We want you to enjoy more fully your spiritual life.

"Connected" encouraged any already existing groups to continue with their style and format. The norm for new groups was to try to "cross-section," that is mix male, female, young, old, married, single. Geographical proximity need not be the criterion for grouping. Special interests, common tasks, and common ministry were encouraged as the natural way of grouping people. The "Connected" team permitted *any* grouping proposed, to accommodate the pluralistic nature of the parish.

The first round of small group meetings was held weekly for seven weeks. After the Lenten-Pentecost season, each group decided how frequently and for how long they would meet.

Deacon Ferrini, parish staff, and "Connected" team members were earnest in choosing pastoral facilitators, or *hosts* for the small communities. Six training sessions ensued, in which Father Art Baranowski's training materials (provided by St. Anthony Messenger) were used. In addition, just before the Lenten groups met, a warm-up session on the basics of small group facilitation was held. A core team for "Connected" continues to be of service to the parish council.

In August 1991, Ferrini sent me an update on the "Connected" process. According to his statistical summary twenty-four "Connected" groups started after the mission. Eleven Little Rock Scripture Study groups already existed. Twelve already existing groups chose to use "Connected" materials. Twenty-five adolescent groups with adult facilitators, called "Quest," merged with "Connected" — all resulting in seventy-one small faith communities, with 889 participants. One of the twenty-four "Connected" groups chose not to continue.

———

Father Richard Ling, pastor of St. Francis Cabrini parish in Littleton, Colorado, is re-forming that parish into a "community of communities." He reminds his parishioners of the meaning of the words *parish* and *diocese*. *Parish* came from two Greek words, *par* and *oikos,* meaning "beyond the house." *Diocese* comes from the two words *dia* and *oikos* and means "cutting across the houses." Thus, both *parish* and *diocese* presume small gatherings of believers within each umbrella term. Ling echoes the findings of the Vatican report *Sects, Cults and New Religious Movements,* which says that many Catholics are leaving Catholic parishes because of the coldness and anonymity. The small groups offered by evangelical and cultic movements are addressing people's need to *belong*. The Vatican report spoke of belonging, love, communication, community, friendship, fellowship, reconciliation, roots, refuge, safety, shelter, and home to describe the intra- and interpersonal experience of small groups. In describing the "small ecclesial communities" that he is trying to facilitate, Ling speaks of them as gatherings of faithful believers that are *dialogical, inclusive, evangelizing,* and characterized by *mutuality*. Ling believes small communities are constitutive of the future of the parish.

Beverly Gibbs-Quintavalle is the coordinator for small faith-sharing communities for the Office for Evangelization in the archdiocese of Minneapolis–St. Paul. After working at the generation of small faith-sharing groups for several years, she reports the following results: of the diocese's 223 parishes, 146 are involved with small groups. Approximately ten thousand people meet in some fashion, with some regularity in small groups. Most groups meet for six weeks in the fall and six weeks in Lent, though some have gone on to much more of a commitment. The Office for Evangelization has produced catechetical-discussion materials for these groups and mailed one free of charge to each pastor or parish contact person. The office gives permission to duplicate the materials to meet parish needs.

Gibbs-Quintavalle is educating the archdiocese about the permanency of small communities, that is, that they are not terminal programs, but ongoing, living cells of parish life. She is also encouraging the leaders of small groups to interact and network with each other. She is assisted by ten advisors, called "the chosen," who set the direction for small communities in the archdiocese. She and "the chosen" have regular gatherings to train pastoral leaders in outreach and the maintenance and nurturance of small faith communities.

---

Sr. Audrey Thomson, R.S.J. is the director of the Australian Promoting Group of Movement for a Better World. She wrote me recently with some reactions to *Re-Imagining the Parish*. In that book I spoke of the Better World Movement as a vital force in sparking small communities around the world. First, she clarified the name or title of the organization. While some speak of "the Better World Movement," Sister clarified that the technical title is Promoting Group of Movement for a Better World. She says,

> We work to promote movement toward ongoing renewal of persons, groups, and structures in society and in the church. Movement toward a Better World was begun in Italy in 1952 by a Jesuit priest, Ricardo Lombardi. He was deeply troubled by the hatred and destruction that he experienced in post–World War II Europe. He began to preach the need for reconciliation and Jesus as *the hope* and *the Savior* of a shattered world. He was supported by Pope Pius XII in beginning a campaign which began the *movement* toward renewal in the church. Priests, religious women, and laity joined him in forming the Promoting Group of Movement for a Better World.

PGMBW has certain principles that provide a summary to this chapter on excellence in small Christian communities. These principles are part of what is called the "New Image of Parish" project.

"New Image of Parish" is about the conversion and renewal of persons and parishes toward genuine community. NIP estimates that most parishes are experienced like a pyramid. Perhaps 25 percent of the typical parish is very involved in community, with only 5 percent in leadership positions or with a high investment. The pyramid ideally would be replaced with a circle of small communities, each connected to each other, each receiving life from the Risen Christ at the center. The goal of NIP is 100 percent participation, not 25 percent. The journey of renewal unfolds in three stages.

The first stage is a call to everyone through regular planned events. This educational-motivational piece concludes with an invitation to all parishioners to meet regularly in small groups. The second stage, through the small groups, is a deeper *discovery together* of Jesus, the Good News, and the meaning of life. The third stage is the maturation of the small groups into Christian communities characterized by *participation* and *communion*.

NIP states emphatically that for these stages to evolve, some specific strategies are needed: (1) the pastoral care of all as community; (2) structures for decision making; (3) structures for communication. NIP states that these three are foundational, and must never be neglected.

The basic NIP decision-making structures are (1) a parish coordinating team; (2) zones, or geographical subdivisions, to make relational participation more possible; (3) a zone coordinating team.

Other key elements include (1) a parish newsletter and editorial team and (2) a network of messengers to deliver the newsletter and be a link of two-way communication in the parish (we will explore this idea in another chapter on evangelical reach-out).

All of the above enable parish leaders to call *all* together in the name of Christ and the parish. The planning of parish educational, liturgical, and social events is done in a steady, ongoing way — sometimes stressing the parish as a whole, other times stressing the zone, or even a smaller cell, the small Christian community. These various structures and strategies are an attempt at pastoral care for *all* as community. All other aspects of parish life are channelled and coordinated through these processes and structures, lending a common direction to all pastoral efforts.

# CHAPTER SEVEN

# St. John Neumann, St. Charles, Ill.: Excellence in Youth Evangelization

Often in the process of teaching, the one being taught goes far beyond the teacher in vision and praxis. Such has been my experience in working with one young man (and others) whom I taught at the Loyola University Institute of Pastoral Studies. One of the courses I teach there is in the area of youth evangelization. The acronym FLAME is used to describe a strategy of youth evangelization that I advocate, an attempt, learned from the evangelical world, to promote a ministerial effort in an upbeat, "not too-churchy" package. The letters stand for key ingredients in a very teleological, that is, purposive process, which will be explained later: F, friendship; L, leadership; A, acceptance; M, Ministry; E, Education.

Many efforts at Catholic youth ministry flounder because they are going nowhere. There is the sporadic dance, ski trip, or other social event. There are the catechetical efforts, often wrapped in the trappings of "schooling." There might be a retreat here or there. Often the numbers of participants are minimal. The youth minister — whether a paid professional or volunteer — has impossible expectations placed on him or her. Of greatest concern, the efforts are splintered or compartmentalized, not united in a meaningful flow toward a goal. There is, in effect, no vision nor goal.

At Loyola I advocate calling young people to *commitment*. I feel we are underwhelming them with our staid, boring approach to church. Perhaps we are excluding them, not inviting them to be a vital, invested part of the experience of church.

I ask students, then, who plan to take on youth ministry as their main ministry to re-imagine youth work as a process. The process is going somewhere — commitment to Christ, the Reign of God, the values of God's Reign, apostleship, and mission to the world. This process may include a ritual or sacramental event, perhaps even confirmation. But it must not be reduced to an anemic confirmation program, filled with legalities, hoops to be jumped through for the sacramental carrot, meaningless service projects, and drab catechesis. Youth evangelization must be re-imagined and then structures created for the continuing journey of initiation. Evangelizing adolescents is to provide a fuller flowering of the meaning of their baptism.

St. John Neumann parish and its youth minister, Frank Mercandante, have taken some of my ideas, merged them with those of others and with their own and have come up with a unique version of FLAME. Their evangelization-initiation process involves confirmation as a ritual of owning one's faith and completing the three ritual moments of initiation: the water bath, the Table, and the sealing with oil and Spirit.

St. John Neumann implements this process amid a flurry of controversy over the appropriate age for confirmation. I am of the opinion that it ought to occur when candidates, sponsors, parents, and parish ministers discern readiness. No age should be assigned it. St. John's believes the developmental readiness for completing initiation can hardly be present before some time in adolescence or young adulthood. I suppose in the ideal order we would suspend infant baptism, have some ritual of welcome into the Christian community at infancy, and engage children, adolescents, and adults in gradual initiation until the point of readiness is discerned. I cannot see the "central office" accepting this notion, so we will all have to continue struggling along pastorally.

St. John's engages in regular, systematic catechesis with the whole congregation, but especially with its young people, on the meaning of initiation. In its catechetical materials, the parish explains that all commitments and relationships take time and need a process.

Building on the vision and praxis of the Order of Christian Initiation, Mercandante and his team have reframed the stages of initiation in a five-step process.

1. *Discovery:* Young people at this stage of the process engage in events and activities that help them discover good times, fun, friends, a relationship with Christ, and the initial experience of Christian community. "Discovery" is made up of monthly social events,

youth center activities, basic training meetings in the skills of peer
ministry, and "Discovery" retreats, which are basic awakening or
evangelization retreats.

2. *Developing Faith as a Lifestyle.* If "Discovery" can be compared to an evangelization period as in the Order of Initiation, this
second stage finds its parallel in the catechumenate proper, or catechesis. In "Developing Faith . . ." adult catechists and peer-to-peer
ministers bring faith to bear on the real-life issues of the world of
the adolescents. These gatherings always use a subjective lens —
the needs and questions of the young people. Common teen issues
are looked at in light of Christian faith. The goal of these events
is deepened commitment and gradual immersion into community.
This stage is comprised of bimonthly "Advance!" small-group catechetical meetings and occasional "Advance!" overnights. The latter
are an adaptation of the retreat format for deepening, catechetical
purposes.

3. *Journeying as a Disciple.* This stage parallels Purification and
Enlightenment, or proximate preparation for sacraments, and focuses
on becoming an intentional disciple of Jesus. The connotation of
"disciple" or "learner" is stressed. During this process, the young people ideally learn (1) to be committed followers of Jesus; (2) what it
means to be Catholic Christians; and (3) to become servant-leaders
like Christ, who led through service.

The commitment at this stage is ever-deepening, as evidenced in
the number and style of meetings. Discipleship meetings are held
every Wednesday. At this stage, those who seriously feel called to commitment move beyond the rudimentary group that they have been in
and into a more spiritually mature discipleship group. St. John's experience embodies the *dynamic* spoken of years ago by both Don
Kimball and Tom Zanzig, pioneers in youth work. True spiritual and communal socialization is best visualized by a wedge. The
deeper the level of discipleship and commitments the fewer the
numbers.

4. *Celebration:* Years ago in *The Book of Sacramental Basics* Tad
Guzie referred to the need we have to celebrate sacraments with integrity. Guzie meant that a sacramental ritual ought to "sign" real-life
change or conversion. One of the pastoral problems haunting the
church is the dishonesty of our sacramental celebrations. So many
"sacramentalized-unevangelized" people say things in ritual that are
in fact not true. They express a "vowing to Christ and commu-

nity," which is what a sacrament in essence is, that really has not been achieved in their lives. Young people in St. John Neumann's FLAME process, to the degree that they are developmentally capable, are very deliberately vowing, borrowing that ancient connotation of *sacrament* from church father Tertullian.

If theologies and ideologies about the proper age of confirmation lead to a parish conflict, that should not require dropping this very important component of a wholistic process of youth evangelization. Whether in the renewal of baptismal vows, the equivalents of a baptism in the Holy Spirit, or some alternative, young people ought to be given the opportunity to publicly own their faith.

5. *Continuing the Journey*. Parallel to the Order of Initiation's Mystagogia, or post-Initiation catechesis, is the postsacramental celebration stage. Rather than confining this to the fifty days between Easter and Pentecost, this period is interpreted more broadly. The sacramental event is not an end but rather a beginning. Opportunities are provided for continued spiritual development, but equally important is aiding young people to hear the call to mission and ministry. Young people are invited into ongoing discipleship groups, to join the Student Ministry Team, or to enter into liturgical ministries.

Frank Mercandante and his staff do their best to emphasize process, discernment, and a nonlegal approach to the sacrament. While certain requirements are present at each stage, adaptation and flexibility are cornerstone principles of this process. Moving toward the celebration stage may involve from two to five years. What is crucial is that both process and sacramental moment are honest and not yet another vehicle of "cheap grace."

FLAME attracts both parochial and public high school youth. For parochial school strategies the parish sees itself in partnership with the school, not in competition, in the forming of disciples. A great deal of enablement and collaborative ministries are needed for this process to work effectively. Both adult and peer ministers are in need of ongoing support and training. Adults might find themselves ministering at different steps of the process: some at the "Discovery" stage, some at the "Advance!" stage, others at the "Discipling" stage, others at the "Continuing..." stage. At each stage, adults might engage in social ministry, evangelization-catechetical ministry, retreat work, spiritual direction, or apprenticing in ministry — all based on young peoples' needs and the charisms of the adults involved.

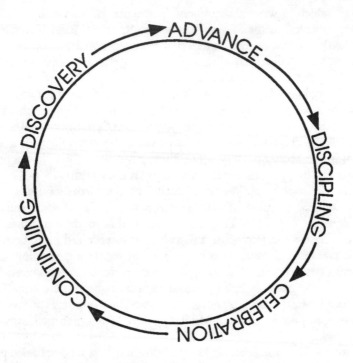

The St. John Neumann's youth evangelization process, then, looks like this: Yearly fall rally to begin youth ministry efforts ⟶ "Discovery" events, meetings and retreat ⟶ "Advance!" events, meetings, and retreats ⟶ "Discipleship" events, meetings, and retreats ⟶ Celebration ⟶ "Continuing the Journey" (through ongoing "Discipleship" groups, student ministry teams, and liturgical ministries).

Keep in mind that students are developmentally in different places throughout this process. Like the process in the Order of Initiation, there may be program pieces, but this is not properly called a "program." Neither is it best imaged linearly. The process is much more like a circle, an ongoing year-long mission of the church.

Besides the genius of the ministerial structure, there is the passionate spirituality that undergirds it. Frank Mercandante knows that the local parish has a responsibility to its young people. That responsibility is not just to run social events, take kids to concerts, bore them with lifeless catechetical materials, or subject them to adult-oriented liturgies. He realizes that what is needed is to make *disciples* of young people. His is a challenging ministry in the anti-gospel culture that young people live in. But he has structures and ministries that effectively fit his mission.

# CHAPTER EIGHT

# Church of the Holy Spirit, Schaumburg, Ill.: Excellence in Televangelization

The Church of the Holy Spirit is a vibrant suburban parish in sprawling Schaumburg, Illinois, a suburb that has become a major city. Once a German farm town, it now sports a skyline, because civic leaders attracted a major shopping mall and many corporate headquarters to what once were fields of wheat and corn. Now twenty years old, the parish is guided still by its founding pastor, Father George Kane. Among Kane's strengths are his pastoral sensitivity, willingness to take innovative risks, and sound theological grounding. He also is ecumenically concerned, and that spirit of ecumenism led him to cooperate with Presbyterian minister Carl Menkens in a project named "Calling in Love."

In fact, Menkens proposed the seminal idea of "Calling in Love" to Father Kane. It is an evangelization campaign accomplished on the telephone, that is, by telemarketing. Carl became the program designer and trainer for the initial round of calls in this Catholic parish. Before discussing the nuts and bolts of the program, we will summarize the convictions on which it is built:

1.  The typical parish is situated in one of the largest mission fields in the world. America is a mission field. Some researchers estimate that there are 96 million people in the United States with no religious affiliation, and another 73 million inactive or nominal

58

Christians. There are only five countries in the world with a total population larger than our unchurched/inactive population.

2. Some of the resistance to the gospel in the 1960s, 1970s, and 1980s is passé. While membership has been declining in mainline Protestant churches, it is growing in the Roman Catholic Church and conservative denominations, according to the National Council of Church's *Yearbook of American and Canadian Churches, 1991*. The five churches showing the greatest membership increase in 1988–89 are, in percentage order:

   * the Presbyterian Church in America (distinct from the Presbyterian Church U.S.A.), up 4.3 percent to 217,374 members;

   * the Roman Catholic Church, up 3.8 percent to 57,019,948 members;

   * the Free Methodist Church of North America, up 3.0 percent to 75,869 members;

   * the Jehovah's Witnesses, up 2.6 percent to 825,570 members;

   * the Christian and Missionary Alliance, up 2.4 percent to 265,863 members.

3. If done in a nonproselytizing, nonmanipulative, dialogical way, people will respond positively when someone calls them on the phone. In fact, the leaders of the "Calling in Love" movement believe that with high crime rates and the busyness of people, the telephone call is a safer, more secure mode of reachout than a home visit. The telephone can provide large-scale, immediate personal contact and dialogue. A phone conversation can plant an evangelical seed that will grow to fruition later.

4. Given the proper training and support, phone calling ministry can be quite rewarding and enjoyable. Many who have tried it in various denominations have stayed with the ministry for a significant period.

The principle behind telemarketing is the transmission of a message to a large number of people in a short time. In the vast missionary territory described earlier, such a call may be the only contact people have with the church or their first positive encounter with a Christian congregation. Telemarketing discerns who among the many called are receptive to contact with the church. Telemarketing makes a church more visible and better known in an area. The entire congregation and the ministering team are moved from simply nurturance and maintenance toward a greater sense of mission. The parish begins to do grassroots research by listening to peoples' needs, feelings, and hurts. As evidenced by the Church of the Holy Spirit's "Calling in Love" campaign, new ministries can arise based on the discerned needs. Telemarketing can be a significant new plan of action in a parish's overall *process* of growth. Better ministries of care, a greater emphasis on the *relational* — not just once or once in a while, but as an ongoing process — will eventually lead to church growth. If more calls are made, the list of potentially receptive people will develop more rapidly.

Ministering in telemarketing can take place in various forms. An evangelization or mission committee can take on the ministry, or a special task force can be formed to do the work. The Church of the Holy Spirit did not have an evangelization or mission committee, so Father Kane and others, through education and recruitment, created a task force.

The "Calling in Love" program says that it is best to have "an occasion" to call, that is, to be able to invite the one called, especially an alienated or unchurched person, to some event. Possibilities include announcing upcoming seasonal programs such as Advent or Lenten activities, the Christmas or Easter schedule, the precatechumenate program, a "back to church" series for the inactive or alienated, or parish social events. Congregations that have used "Calling in Love" have found various adaptations and applications of the process arise for their situation and needs.

It is crucial to keep in mind the real purpose of telemarketing: to surface receptive people, people at a point in their lives in which they are, perhaps unconsciously, on a spiritual quest. Real ministry begins once the receptive have been surfaced. It would be counterproductive and perhaps even more alienating not to do follow-up ministry with those discerned as "receptive."

Menkens and other leaders in "Calling in Love" efforts strongly suggest the following ministries in such a missionary project:

1. the project coordinator: a staff member or able lay leader;

2. the telephone team leader: the person responsible for recruiting, training, and scheduling the telephone calling team;

3. the budget manager: the one who manages the finances needed and used;

4. the publicity director: the person who produces promotional material, educating people about the campaign and ministry, and also follow-up materials to be sent to those discerned as "receptive" during the initial phone call;

5. the welcome coordinator: the one who, through a variety of means, provides hospitality to the "receptive" who take a step toward participation, investigation, or experimentation with the congregation.

At the Church of the Holy Spirit, by special arrangement with Illinois Bell, ten phone jacks were installed in the lower level of the parish center. The lines can be turned on and off upon request depending on whether a phone call campaign is underway. At the liturgies and through the mail as many people as possible — parishioners and non-parishioners — were informed and educated about the process. Using the services of Donnelly Press, the company that prints phone books for the Chicago metropolitan area, some eleven hundred names, addresses, and phone numbers were assembled during the summer of 1990. These were not all Catholic homes or units, but rather the names of all people, of any faith or no faith, living within the geographical boundaries of the parish. The first round of activity was to mail to all these homes with bulk-rate postage information about "Calling in Love" and also "Search for God," the Church of the Holy Spirit's adult faith formation series open to all. Recruitment then followed for the group to undergo training to call the eleven hundred. Over one hundred parishioners came forward. *All* parishioners, however, were encouraged to be conscious of and pray for the effort.

Training was done in one session, held at different times, to accommodate callers' schedules. The "soft scripting" that was given callers had a simple focus: (1) to identify if the person or household called were churched; (2) if not, to determine if they would like some printed material that would give them more information on the parish. The actual calling was done Monday through Friday for four weeks during July and August, from 6:00 P.M. to 9:00 P.M. Several Sunday evenings were also used. A schedule of *who* was calling *when* was sent to all callers. The role of a weekly coordinator was created. The person was to fill in and make phone calls during periods not covered by the other volunteers. Babysitting was provided for those who needed it to fulfill their commitment to call. A bilingual parishioner was recruited to call the Hispanic people.

These one hundred plus volunteers made 8,700 phone calls from the list of almost 11,000. Almost 1,000 of those called expressed an interest in more information about Holy Spirit, which was promptly mailed to them. The mailing was followed up within two weeks with another round of phone calls. Deacon Ray Doud, who eventually became the director of the project, admits that there were omissions in some of the follow-up calls, with volunteers losing interest or not having enough time. Nonetheless, throughout 1990–91, some 980 people regularly received phone calls and printed material regarding Advent, Christmas, Easter, and a special new ministry that flowed from "Calling in Love": " Once a Catholic."

"Calling in Love" had some immediate results. "Search for God" had its biggest attendance in its history, over 120 people. A process of return-rebirth was begun. People came to the parish center to register as a result of the phone call of days or weeks past. The phone call planted an evangelical time bomb that went off later. Perhaps most importantly the consciousness of both callers and the entire congregation began to change — from maintenance to mission and world orientation.

The phone calls stopped for awhile at Church of the Holy Spirit. The first round in 1990 stirred enough people needing ministry and new programs that there was not time or energy to continue en masse calling. Having responded fairly well to people surfaced in the first round, now, over a year later, the Church of the Holy Spirit is ready to start again. New names, needs, and ministries will appear. Father Kane is proceeding slowly, cautiously, but with consistency and determination.

Among the ministries that have flowed from the "Calling in Love" effort is "Once a Catholic," coordinated by George Kane and pastoral associate Dawn Mayer, who also is the codirector of evangelization efforts in Chicago with me. "Once a Catholic" is a flexible process created for Catholics who are experiencing a call or awakening back to church participation after a period of distancing or estrangement.

Following the example of Msgr. Thomas Cahalane (see chapter 12), Kane and Mayer use Christmas and Easter as special opportunities, not to chide Christmas-Easter Catholics, but rather to welcome them, inviting them to a six-part inquiry series. The Church of the Holy Spirit issued the Christmas-Easter invitation three times, attracting thirty people the first time, twenty-seven the second, and nineteen the third.

Dawn reports that the group seems to attract two kinds of people: the truly alienated (those hurt or angry with the church) and those being led to church participation by the emerging spiritual needs of their children. Kane and Mayer are finding a need to separate the two groups because they are different — with anger and hurt on the one hand and curiosity and interest on the other. The sessions begin with participants anonymously submitting questions and issues to the team for discussion. Every session then focuses on one or more of the issues. Toward the middle of each process, participants are asked what their fondest memories of the church from the past are. They are also asked to do some "futuring": what role do they hope to play in the church, specifically their parish, in the future.

Some former participants in "Once a Catholic" have become members of the team for a future process. For all who have gone through "Once a Catholic," there are reunions every couple of months. George and Dawn report that in each of the three offerings most of the participants have returned to church and Eucharist by the end of the process. A weakness they have confessed is the absence of meaningful rituals, like those that are part of the "Re-Membering Church" process at St. Ephrem's in Sterling Heights, Michigan (see chapter 12). Dawn and George did experiment with a "gathering around the baptismal font," a ritual for reaffirming baptismal vows, at the end of one "Once a Catholic" series.

The "Calling in Love" and "Once a Catholic" series are further supplemented by the distribution to every house within the geographical boundaries of the parish. The bimonthly newspaper *Information from*... produced by the Paulist Evangelization Office, was alluded to before. Though distributing this to every household is a heavy expense, it has given even greater visibility to Church of the Holy Spirit. As in all marketing efforts, printed material has greater impact on some people than others.

"Calling in Love" has flowed into two other ministries besides "Once a Catholic" and *Information from.*... Dawn Mayer and other team members, realizing that most young couples coming to the parish are "sacramentalized but unevangelized," have started an initiation-like process for marriage preparation. At least six months prior to their wedding, a couple begins meeting with a mentoring couple around the key issues of marriage, especially marriage as a sacrament. The mentoring couple companions the soon-to-be married couple right up to the rehearsal. Of great significant is a public rite of engagement, which parallels the Order of Initiation's Rite of Election. At some point in the process of moving toward vows, the couples are both introduced to the Sunday assembly and ritually move into proximate preparation for marriage.

Finally there is the welcoming ministry, which includes the visitation of newcomers to the parish, with various symbols of welcome, an explanation of the parish mission statement, and invitations to involvement. It resembles the welcoming process in another parish, St. Thomas the Apostle in Naperville, Illinois (see the next chapter). In both instances, and in other examples we will share, the commandment is "thou shalt not register a new parishioner with a parish secretary." Too often that newcomer becomes a name on a card in a drawer — functionally alienated or unchurched. Welcoming ministries are really attempts to prevent church alienation.

The Church of the Holy Spirit: truly an excellent parish, taking risks in innovative attempts at evangelizing.

# CHAPTER NINE

# St. Thomas the Apostle, Naperville, Ill.; Holy Family, Inverness, Ill.: Excellence in Welcoming the Stranger

One of the things that we do least well in the Catholic experience is welcome newcomers. Too often registration is with the parish secretary. The name is placed on a card, in a drawer, and most of such folks eventually join the inactive or the liturgically active but socially and ministerially uninvolved categories. Two congregations in the suburbs of Chicago stand out as communities trying to overcome the "poor welcoming" syndrome. One is in the diocese of Joliet (St. Thomas the Apostle, Naperville), the other in the archdiocese of Chicago (Holy Family, Inverness).

Registration at St. Thomas's is held after liturgy on the weekends. Folks can also stop in at the parish center during the week. Registration is explained as a concrete way to express one's commitment to the parish faith community. Though parish boundaries are part of canon law, all the parishes in Naperville (six as of this writing) have agreed to allow people to register wherever they feel most comfortable and where they can grow spiritually.

The official meeting with a parish staff member or administrative assistant is quickly followed up with a home visit. A team of parishioners, most trained in human relationships skills, visit all new parishioners with a handsome portfolio of materials. The trained ministers are called "welcome ministers." In the folder are included the following:

1. A letter from the current pastor, Father Jim Curtain. The tone of the letter is inviting and welcoming, but also theological. He develops a wholistic spirituality of stewardship, explaining that it involves sharing not only one's funds, but also time, gifts, and charisms — for the common good and the glory of God.

2. A brief statement on the sacramental life of the parish, dividing the seven sacraments into "sacraments of initiation," "sacraments of healing," and the "social sacraments," of matrimony and holy orders.

3. A sheet on the process of marriage preparation, which resembles the process at the Church of the Holy Spirit in Schaumburg. Here also matrimony follows a catechumenal model, with companion couples journeying with the engaged through their rehearsal and celebration.

4. A sheet to explain the Order of Initiation, in case anyone in the family might be interested in joining the church.

5. A statement on the importance of baptism, not only to inform parents of infants, but to highlight for all the centrality of baptism for the Catholic Christian.

6. Lists of ministries and leadership committees are provided. How to get involved in ministry or leadership is explained. The ministries represented include liturgy, religious education, pastoral care, social concerns, youth, music, development and fundraising, adult continuing education, and Christian initiation.

7. A sheet explaining the church's building and environment. The sheet describes the theology or spirituality of the artifacts and why they are placed where they are. Those included are the baptismal font, the Table, the ambo, the celebrant's chair, the tabernacle, and the sanctuary lamp. People are thus aided in understanding a proper reverence for the Word, the Table, the presider, the presanctified Eucharist, and the centrality of baptism. Art objects are also explained: the statue of Mary, the rose window, the Stations of the Cross, the Resurrection Cross, and the stained-glass windows.

8. A list of the staff, offering personal and biographical material on each, with an accompanying picture. Included are the pastor, the associate pastor, the deacon, the pastoral associates, the director of liturgy and music, the youth minister, and the director of religious education.

9. An updated calendar of social events, welcoming people, not just to the parish's tasks and ministries, but also its social life, parties, and celebrations. Examples from a recent year include:

   • January: Progressive Dinner

   • March: Parish Theme Dance

   • April: Las Vegas Night

   • May: Women's Luncheon

   • July: Parish Picnic

   • September: Children Fest

10. A very clear map on how to get to the parish. In the ever-expanding town of Naperville this is provided to help newcomers develop a rootedness in the complex of winding streets.

In recent months a new development has taken place. A brief video on the parish has been made to supplement the written material. If the parish visitor notices a VCR in the home visited, he or she may ask if the video can be played during the visit.

An envelope is included in the packet with the words "To serve the Lord...Our Call to Stewardship." After the home visitor's explanation of the parish, the hope is that the newcomer will respond by sharing time, talent, charism, and treasure.

Unlike many one-shot home visitation programs, St. Thomas's program makes provision for follow-up. Each visitor or welcome minister must complete a visitation report with recommendations for follow-up.

Following the skills of "andragogy," that is, adult learning theory, outlined in *Re-Imagining the Parish*, St. Thomas's regularly listens to the needs of parishioners and provides programming, especially adult education and enrichment, based on those needs. The most recent survey analyzed sex, age, marital status, length of time in the parish, children living at home, level of parish participation, the nature

## VISITATION REPORT

Name: _____

Address: _____

Area/Subdivision: _____

Telephone (Home) _____ Work _____

*(on the other side of the card )*

1. Did you find any need for staff involvement?

   Which staff person??

   Need:

2. Comments:

3. What are your impressions after the visit?

   Will become involved:

   Needs encouragement to become involved:

   Will not be involved in my opinion:

Welcome minister's name:

---

of children's participation in religious education programs, the aspects of St. Thomas's that most positively influence one's life, trends in the neighborhood that the parish ought to be aware of, desirable new programs or ministries, and things that ought to be changed to improve St. Thomas's. This most recent need discernment resulted in a new staff position and ongoing discussion about an additional one. Father Curtain and the parish leadership community have hired a full-time credentialed pastoral counselor. Almost immediately this religious sister's schedule was full, and it continues to be. People feel a need to look at personal and relational issues through both psychotherapeutic and spiritual lenses.

In addition, the parish is discerning whether it should hire a coordinator for spiritual development and retreats. The focus of this person's ministry would be to help parishioners with their "inner

## PRAYER FOR
## ST. THOMAS THE APOSTLE PARISH

*Creator God, You have given us life, made us in your image, and breathed your Spirit into us. We acknowledge that you have placed within our hearts a deep need and hunger to know you and to share in your love. We come before you in a spirit of peace and trust, asking you for all that we need.*

*Loving and gracious God, our lives are often pushed and pulled by hundreds of activities. In the busy pace of life, we realize the need to come in touch with the deeper meaning of life.*

*God of Light and Wisdom, we need you. We need a clear vision, a deep understanding, a broad perspective. Free us from the fears and pressures, both from within and without, that keep us from discovering that you are the answer to our deepest yearnings. Gift us with the spirit of openness and generosity, as we walk with each other as companions on the journey, seeking ways to bring the "good news" to all. Help us to recognize you as you reveal yourself to us, to hear you as you speak to us in the events of our daily lives, in Eucharist and prayer, and in each other. You are inviting us and calling us. Let us respond with eagerness and joy.*

*God of strength and source of all life, guide us in our efforts to create community at St. Thomas's Parish. Awaken in us too, the courage to reach out to the wounded and powerless and poor in our midst.*

*St. Thomas the Apostle, we pray with you in a spirit of deep faith.*

*Holy Mary, Mother of God, we honor you and thank you for your intercession for us to your Son, Jesus Christ, who daily blesses us with good gifts.*

*Amen!*

work," conversion and transformation of life. People said that they wanted to learn more about faith, about God's presence in human experience, about Scripture, about couple's spirituality, about eucharistic theology, and about spiritual healing. The new staff member would be responsible for retreat programs and spiritual direction that helps with these issues.

━━━━━

In the archdiocese of Chicago, Holy Family Parish, an innovative community started in 1984 by current pastor Father Medard Laz, is a beehive of Catholic activity close to the Willowcreek Community megachurch mentioned earlier. As part of its welcoming process, this parish also has developed a brochure containing a description of Holy Family's history, a Time and Talent Sheet, a facility floor plan (so that newcomers can find their way around the elaborate multipurpose complex), a biography of the pastor, the parish's mission statement, and a list of Holy Family traditions, which include:

- greeters at the doors of the church and the exchange of greetings among parishioners at the beginning of Eucharist;

- the wearing of name badges to foster community;

- the use of special lighting effects, music, slides, and drama to bring alive the Liturgy of the Word;

- spontaneous petitions from the assembly at Sunday gatherings;

- an extended greeting of peace during the liturgy, highlighting the importance of real-life reconciliation before communion;

- mentioning one's name at the reception of communion, to make the experience more personalized;

- hospitality after the liturgy in the large narthex.

Newcomers who express interest in the parish receive the following letter from the pastor.

Welcome to Holy Family Parish Community! We are delighted that you have found us and you are interested in joining our community.

We feel that we have something most special here — a warm, close, and friendly group of believers who have accepted the Lord into their life, and as a result of this, truly care about and minister to those in our community and beyond.

Because of this I ask that you attend several of our Masses at Holy Family to get to know us and we you. Our Masses and our spirit are different from other parishes. You may discuss with your family your commitment to the parish in the following areas:

1. Attend Mass each week at Holy Family,

2. Get involved with one of our many ministries, and

3. Offer your fair share of financial support.

When you are ready to make your commitment, call the parish office at 359-0042 to set up a time to register. Upon registration you will receive additional information about our parish community. You will also be informed of our welcoming process, which we expect our new parishioners to participate in to learn of our vision, our history, and our goals. Registration and participation are a matter of covenant to us so that we can continue to build a strong and even more vibrant faith community.

I am thrilled that you have become aware of us and, as you will often hear me say, "See you Sunday at the Lord's table."

With warm wishes,
Fr. Medard Laz

The committee that has devised the welcoming process was made up of Father Rich Yanos, John and Marie Chlopecki, Nancy Lacek, Peggy Molohan, and Anne Spain. The two goals of the process are to improve welcoming and to reaffiliate inactive members, who, for whatever motivation, may be registering at Holy Family. Though the process has been reshaped over the months, the original plan was to invite newcomers to a four-part welcoming series as follows:

1. *Night One: Welcome! Welcome! Welcome!* At this session participants are encouraged to tell a little of their stories after team members share theirs, as well as the story of Holy Family.

2. *Night Two: Understanding Your Catholic Faith.* This session is a teaching opportunity. Though the word *ecclesiology* is not used, that is the focus. The relationship between universal church and

the local parish, Holy Family, is discussed, as well as the unique nature of Holy Family — a parish comprised of people who have moved to it from around the country. Other issues brought in during the "church" session are contemporary understandings of sacraments, spirituality, morality and liturgy, and the goals appropriate for Holy Family members.

3. *Night Three: Understanding Your Commitment to Holy Family.* This session focuses on the gifts and charisms of newcomers and how these gifts can be used for the glory of God and the common good. Again an ecclesiology stressing the connectedness between universal and local church is employed. This is a very important insight in a parish of high mobility. My research into alienated, nonpracticing Catholics has revealed that a sort of "congregational Catholicism," where one cannot see beyond one's own parish, contributes to the drop-out syndrome.

4. *Night Four: Where Do We Go from Here?* In this session group leaders discuss practical ways of involvement, but also the larger issue of whether the newcomers — through registration — are ready to make a public commitment to Holy Family Parish.

The Holy Family welcoming process is an attempt to give potential new members a catechumenate-like journey toward committing resources and self to the parish. Its process nature is much more likely to create engaged parish members than the "signing the card" approach. I know of an Episcopal parish that has taken the process a step further and added a public ritual at a weekend gathering. After a process of assimilating and deciding to invest in the vision of the congregation, newcomers make a public commitment to parish membership in the context of the worshipping community.

One caution I would place on all such welcoming models is to avoid any trappings of *legalism*. If newcomers, especially if they are nonpracticing or alienated, interpret a catechumenal process of welcoming as no more than a new set of legal hoops church bureaucrats are throwing at them, such welcoming attempts will backfire and aggravate the alienation or anger that the welcomers wanted to heal.

# CHAPTER TEN

## St. Andrew the Apostle, Chandler, Ariz.; St. Clare, St. Denis, Chicago: Excellence in Pastors Creating Pastors

While Father Joseph Hennessey established St. Andrew the Apostle parish almost six years ago in Chandler, Arizona, he, with the help of pioneer parishioners, tried to establish the vision and mission of the parish as *Welcoming, Caring, and Sharing*. Sister Theresa Jodocny, O.S.B., joined the staff in 1987, and most recently Sister Pat Smith. Working with many others they have put together an exciting neighborhood ministry. I see their ministry as "the pastor sharing the pastoring with the baptized." Before going into the details of their process, let me set the stage theologically and theoretically.

In recent years, several significant documents were issued that struck me in their convergence of vision. *The Unchurched American 1988*, issued by the Gallup organization, characterized many mainline churches as suffering the crisis of "believing vs. belonging" — referring to people who have a notional adherence to a faith tradition with little or no direct involvement in a congregation or parish. One of Gallup's suggestions for mainline churches is to get more serious about outreach, personal contact, home visitation.

In a refreshingly honest yet unofficial statement from the bishops of Alta Baja, California, in the spring of 1990, the authors advocate principles similar to Gallup's. In a *A Pastoral Response to Proselytism*, the bishops wrestle with the phenomenon of the many Catholics in their area leaving their church of origin (Roman Catholic) for evangelical churches. They honestly confess that typical Catholic parishes currently have structures inadequate for evangelization. The bishops' suggestions are simple and concrete:

1.  The typical parish needs to be divided into sectors with deacons, deacon couples, or trained laity overseeing them.

2.  The sectors should be further subdivided into small Christian communities, with the baptized trained to pastor or shepherd each other in that context.

3.  Joined to these two efforts should be regular, consistent home visitation.

A third resource echoing some of these same themes is the *National Plan for Hispanic Ministry* (1987), which spoke of the needless fragmentation of ministries in the typical Catholic parish. It recommends a convergence, a collaboration of ministries around the central mission of evangelization. Further specifying, it also recommends the proliferation of small Christian communities and conversion from a "pew mentality" to a "shoes mentality," referring to the need for more pew sitters to realize they must become God's missionaries, sent to the streets and the homes of the parish to invite and welcome others. Similar recommendations have come from the National Black Catholic Congress, and also various convocations concerning the evangelization of Asian immigrants to America.

In summary, the canonically appointed pastor and his numerically small staff cannot be expected to pastor well the vast number of Catholics in most parishes. Parishioners in the future, must, in a variety of ways, pastor each other. The parishes represented in this chapter, however haltingly, are attempting to do this.

———

The neighborhood ministry process at St. Andrew's began with the goal of moving toward small base communities. The staff and other leaders stressed the development of the social life of various neighborhoods of the parish. After establishing fairly sound relationships in the neighborhood groups, Sister Theresa attempted to redirect the focus of the groups toward Scripture sharing. By 1990, there were Scripture sharing groups in six of the eighteen neighbor-hood subgroups. Ideally all eighteen will have this opportunity soon. Much pastoral care takes place within the neighborhood groups. The staff admits that they have only scratched the surface of what could be a more fully developed neighborhood ministry process.

Some of my students at Chicago's Loyola Institute of Pastoral Studies passionately resist any talk of structures when it comes to pastoral renewal. I remind them that without structures, there is no delivery system. Structure, as such, is not the problem. The prob-lem is rather structures that no longer fit the mission. Structures that hold a mission captive rather than structures that congruently fit a mission are a primary pastoral problem. In this light, let us look at the organization of St. Andrew's neighborhood ministry.

---

**Organization of Neighborhood Communities**

The Pastor
Directors of Neighborhoods (Sr. Theresa, Sr. Pat)
Steering Committee
Coordinators and Co-coordinators
Committees Working with Coordinators and Co-coordinators

| | |
|---|---|
| Spiritual Life | Mailing |
| Phoning Committee | Social events |
| Newsletter | General: help when needed |

---

Large group events are held with nearby "sister" neighbor-hoods. The coordinators and co-coordinators of neighborhoods meet monthly as a large community for communication and sharing.

St. Andrew's articulates its mission in this way:

> The Neighborhood Program is designed to bring the gospel message, exemplified by Jesus Christ, into each neighborhood community. This program should enable all persons to experi-ence prayer, welcoming, caring, and sharing on the local level as members of their faith community, which is part of the great parish family of St. Andrew the Apostle. Aware that the church is the people of God in all neighborhoods, members are called by their baptism to build the Reign of God in service to one another.

Each neighborhood tries to surface leadership dedicated to this mission. The emerging leaders are an extension of the parish to the people in the area and also a conduit of communication back to the central parish offices. In each neighborhood attempts are made to raise consciousness that all the baptized are called to ministry and evangelization. Conversation is encouraged at neighborhood gatherings about how all of God's people are gifted, have charisms, and are called to serve.

The following committees are present in each neighborhood; they are crucial for the neighborhood's functioning:

1. *Spiritual Development*, which supports and encourage:

   - Scripture sharing groups

   - sponsors for the Order of Initiation

   - neighborhood sacramental celebrations in collaboration with the directors of religious education

   - Masses in homes

   - other resources, besides Scripture, for adult enrichment and catechesis

   - days of retreat or recollection for the neighborhood

2. *Pastoral Support*, which supports and encourages:

   - visiting the sick from the neighborhood, in their homes, hospitals, or nursing homes

   - distribution of meals to needy families

   - assistance to people dealing with newborn care, prolonged illness of a loved one, death and grieving, or any other special needs

   - aid to the unemployed or economically deprived in the neighborhood.

3. *Social Events*, which supports and encourages:

   - opportunities for each neighborhood to gather for friendship and hospitality

   - larger parish efforts that foster bondedness

- opportunities for children to see adults in healthy friend-
ships and communities, and, in turn, to do the same among
themselves

- car-pooling, child care, and celebration of special days in the
lives of adults and children

- cooperation with the other committees.

4. *Education*, which supports and encourages:

- suggestions on how to strengthen the faith and family life
or single life in each neighborhood

- cooperation with the staff especially in educational opportunities for those in bereavement or processes of separation
or divorce

- the use of the parish central library for enrichment.

Notice how the neighborhood process is not another program
piled upon many other programs. The whole parish has been re-
imagined and ministries have been reshaped around the small church,
or neighborhood.

The *directors* oversee the process in collaboration with the pastor
and steering committee. The directors are key in discerning who from
the neighborhood should be on the steering committee. Neighborhood leaders turn to the directors for leadership themselves. The
directors and steering committee need to work in a friendly and
collaborative manner to provide direction to the neighborhood process. The director also works with others in evaluating the ongoing
development of the neighborhood process.

The *steering committee* meets monthly with the directors and pastor to plan for the weeks and months ahead. The steering committee
also is responsible for assisting in the training of emerging leaders
in the neighborhoods. The steering committee discerns a chairperson who works directly with the pastor and director in planning the
monthly meetings, preparing monthly and yearly calendars, overseeing plans for major neighborhood functions, and serving as contact
persons between the director and other leaders. The steering committee is responsible for replacing members from the neighborhoods
when it becomes a necessity. It deals with pastoral problems that
arise in the flow of the neighborhood's life together and renegotiates
boundary reorganization when necessary.

*Neighborhood coordinators* are trained by appropriate members of the steering committee. They ideally remain in position for two years to provide a sense of continuity in leadership. They should be fully educated and formed in the mission statement's vision and practical goals. They are to find someone to assist in their duties and also to assume leadership in their absence. They also must attend monthly meetings. They can seek advice from assigned steering committee members on the nature of their neighborhood programs and ministries.

The coordinators conduct a yearly organizational meeting in their neighborhood, usually in the fall, to organize a telephone committee, plan functions for the year, and discern leaders for each of the committees.

Coordinators must be involved "hands-on" with the telephone committee, assuring the proper pastoral tone is communicated in this reach-out ministry. The coordinators are responsible for organizing all publicity in the neighborhood (e.g., mailings and bulletin announcements) about neighborhood functioning. The coordinators are vehicles of two-way communication between the neighborhood and central parish offices and staff. They are responsible for welcoming all newcomers in their neighborhood.

The St. Andrew's staff are honest in admitting that their dreams outstrip the reality of their project. But their vision and goals are well thought out and, I believe, exemplary for anyone concerned about better "pastoral coverage" and greater emphasis on "the relational" in parish life.

———

Back in the archdiocese of Chicago, we turn to another model of pastoring in the St. Clare's "Neighbor-to-Neighbor" program begun several years ago. St. Clare de Montefalco historically was a working class parish of European ancestral roots. Much has occurred in recent months to change both the demography of the area and the impact of this ministry. Former pastor Father Jim Friedl, an Augustinian long associated with Marriage Encounter, was the visionary behind "Neighbor-to-Neighbor." The mission statement worked on by staff and congregation speaks of "the warmth and care of Jesus" that must be transmitted now in a parish that "loves and serves all people...in laughter, at times in tears...in our rich Catholic tradition as a hospitable, caring, and warm people."

"Neighbor-to-Neighbor" divided the parish into thirty-eight districts, each district corresponding to two city blocks. A district contains thirty to thirty-five registered households, or about ninety individuals. Each district has a district coordinator who works with four or five other parishioners on the District Telephone Committee. These people maintain regular contact with the parishioners of their district to inform them of parish activities as well as to discern district needs and the gifts that the members of the district have to meet these needs.

"Neighbor-to-Neighbor" is based on the following beliefs:

* Everyone in the community has the right to know what is happening in the parish all the time.

* Everyone is gifted by God.

* We are all called to use our gifts to build up the parish, the neighborhood, and the world.

* The celebration of the Eucharist is enhanced when we are more aware of one another and our gifts.

St. Clare's "Neighbor-to-Neighbor" was advertised through parish mailings to all registered parishioners. All parishioners were given opportunities to lead. The process got off to an exciting start, but soon ran into problems. As has happened throughout most of the south side of Chicago, racial-ethnic minorities began to move into St. Clare's, and many in the mostly white neighborhood joined the white flight to the suburbs. And so "Neighbor-to-Neighbor" never took hold.

Several parishes to the south, St. Denis's has developed a neighborhood ministry program. My associate Dawn Mayer and I conducted a four-part training series, equipping over 150 St. Denis's parishioners with basic human relation skills, like active listening, empathy, effective questioning, and nondefensive responses to criticism against the parish or church. The first round of neighborhood ministers' responsibilities included a parish census. With that completed, the ministers have taken on a more defined job description. Four times a year, neighborhood ministers take a newsletter to the people assigned to them. Though resembling a parish bulletin, it is much more expansive, including information about all aspects of parish activities for several months. The presumption is that such information, well known to active parishioners, is not readily accessible to the many inactive who do not read parish bulletins or hear pulpit announcements.

Neighborhood ministry at St. Denis's was part of the vision of Father John Spitkovsky, who determined that he and his staff could not be as accessible to parishioners and neighborhoods as they should. He invited us in to do training. John died of heart disease before the training began. Perhaps his chronic weakness alerted him to the limits a typical staff faces. Excitement about neighborhood ministry among parishioners is a tribute to him. Father Jim Hagan, John's successor, has continued and refined neighborhood ministry. Unlike in St. Clare's, where neighborhood ministry began to erode with neighborhood change, St. Denis's Neighborhood Ministry seems to have contributed to neighborhood stability and gradual neighborhood integration.

# CHAPTER ELEVEN

# Ascension Parish, Virginia Beach, Va.: Excellence in Catechumenal Vision

In his pioneering work *The Book of Sacramental Basics*, Tad Guzie proposed a vision of sacramental catechesis and faith formation for the future. His basic insight is that the steps of the Order of Initiation are so effective and so integral that they should not be reserved to those first joining the church, but also should become the staple for all engaged in any stage of faith formation or sacramental catechesis. Those rudimentary steps, which can be applied or adapted for all age groups and circumstances, are as follows:

A Time for General Inquiry ⟶ A Rite of Beginning ⟶ A Time for Suitable Catechesis ⟶ A Rite of Proximate Preparation ⟶ A Time for Discipleship ⟶ Vowing/Integral Celebration of All Sacraments ⟶ Postsacramental Faith Formation

This vision is oriented toward the Order of Christian Initiation of Adults, but is applicable to all sacraments and with adaptation can be a paradigm for religious education in general.

Ascension Parish is one of several parishes (St. Nicholas's is another) in the Richmond diocese that not only "started the catechumenate" some years ago, but also actually lives out a catechumenal vision. In the words of one priest who works in the diocese: "Every parish should be in an ongoing posture of precatechumenate; and the stages of initiation are like a jump-rope that the parish continually spins. People jump in when they are ready." Ascension is one of the parishes, led by pastoral visionaries who have implemented these words.

"Emmaus II" is the title that Ascension, under the leadership of Father Bob French and now Father Bill Dale, chose to encompass its total religious education process. Just as the first disciples came to recognize Jesus as they walked the journey of life, it is the hope of Fran Woodward, director of religious education, and all who staff and minister at Ascension that eventually all involved in faith formation — for whatever reason, need, obligation, or interest — will come to recognize Jesus in their unique life journey.

"Emmaus II" includes the following catechumenal processes:

* *Adult Formation:* throughout the year multiple opportunities are offered adults, based on discerned needs of the adult congregation and the parish mission statement.

* *Young Peoples' Faith Formation:* This is the religious education process for grades one through six. The sessions are held on Wednesday from 4:30 to 6:30 P.M. Three times during the year, parents also participate with their children in a formational experience. YPFF concludes with a family eucharistic celebration in the Easter season.

* *Young People's Liturgy of the Word:* YPLW is celebrated at the 8:45 and 11:45 A.M. liturgies. "Breaking Open the Word" is offered for kindergarten through fifth grade. After their own Liturgy of the Word, children join their families for the Liturgy of the Eucharist.

* *Order of Christian Initiation of Adults:* The process of inquiry, formation, proximate preparation, vowing, and ongoing faith formation is offered year round in an ongoing catechumenal process. This means that there are several rituals of acceptance or welcome into the Order of Initiation. As advocated in Thomas Morris's book *RCIA: Transforming the Church*, the process of initiation at Ascension resembles a circular rather than a linear model.

* *Re-Membering Church:* Parallel to the stages and steps of the Order of Initiation is a process of return and rebirth for those who have drifted from the church. Based on the church's ancient Order of Penitents, in which reconciliation was both process and ritual event, "Re-Membering Church" provides returnees

with the time, relationships, communal involvement, and rituals needed for reconciliation. This process is considered more in depth in another chapter.

- *Adult Confirmation:* Adult Catholics who have been active in faith, but have not been confirmed are welcomed to complete their initiation after a process of preparation.

- *Adolescent Faith Formation.* This process is anchored in a celebration of the sacrament of confirmation.

  - In *Stage One* seventh, eight, ninth, and tenth graders concentrate on doctrinal formation, Scripture, prayer, and human development.

  - *Stage Two* is the year of immediate preparation for the celebration of the sacrament of confirmation. It focuses on the spiritual formation of the candidates. Group learning, reflection sessions, sharing sessions with sponsors, retreats, and apostolic service projects are features of this stage.

  - *Stage Three* is the postconfirmation journey. It provides time, support, and a solid group process with adult leaders, so that the young person may more fully absorb the substance of Christian life.

- *Sacraments of Initiation Course.* This four-part series is offered three times a year, fall, winter, and spring. It is an opportunity for adults to renew their own understanding and experience of faith as their children approach one of the sacraments of initiation or the sacrament of reconciliation. The course is oriented toward helping parents prepare their children for one of the four sacraments. To participate in the course, parents must have been registered in the parish for at least three months, should regularly worship and be active in the parish, and be registered in the "Emmaus II" family faith formation process.

  Baptism is celebrated six times a year at the regularly scheduled liturgies. First Reconciliation can be celebrated at a regular Saturday celebration, by a private appointment, or at the seasonal Advent or Lenten communal services. First Eucharist can be celebrated at any regularly scheduled liturgy, except during Lent and the six weekends reserved for baptism.

• *Rainbows* is a social and faith-formational process oriented toward senior citizens. The goal of the process is to encourage seniors to experience themselves as recipients of God's unconditional love for all and to respond to that love faithfully. Seniors, to borrow a term from James Fowler, serve as the guarantors for the community of the reality of God's love and the community's responsibility to respond to God and each other with mutuality.

The energizing force behind much of the religious education of the parish is Fran Woodward.

Like many of the parishes that we have studied, Ascension operates out of a vision of baptismal spirituality, emphasizing the charisms and gifts of all the baptized. As people are welcomed into the parish and later on a regular basis, they are both invited into ministry and also given the proper training for ministry. Here we provide examples of forms on which newcomers or seasoned parishioners could express interest in a particular ministry.

Holy Family parish, whose welcoming process we already studied, borrowed two techniques from Ascension. In a spirit of "model innovation," representatives from Holy Family travelled to Virginia Beach to study their "Emmaus II" process, and other aspects of parish life. "Emmaus II" at Ascension gave birth to FAITH at Holy Family (Faith Alive in the Home). The thrust of FAITH is to place as much of the responsibility for catechesis as possible in the home. Thus, children are catechized in the home or among clusters of families.

Ascension also passed on to Holy Family its tradition of audiovisual assistance (slides, music) to enhance the Liturgy of the Word. Holy Family's use of name tags to foster greater community was also an Ascension idea.

Ascension is among a cluster of parishes in the Richmond diocese that have built their parishes on catechumenal vision. Under the enabling leadership of Bishop Walter Sullivan, these pioneering pastors and their staffs have not allowed the Order of Initiation to be reduced to a weekly instruction program for "converts." These visionaries long ago saw the Order of Initiation as a way of re-imaging and doing church. When implemented properly and adapted for other ministries with pastoral sensitivity, the Rite of Christian Initiation of Adults is the most important document to flow from Vatican II. It is a paradigm for most pastoral ministry and faith formation. Its dynamics even provide a blueprint for basic Christian communities.

# CHURCH OF THE ASCENSION

An open assembly of Catholic believers of the Diocese of Richmond
proclaiming the Word of God, celebrating the Eucharist,
and serving the local community

Name: _____

Address: _____ Telephone: _____

## LITURGICAL MINISTRIES

Worship is the primary activity in which this community participates. Our gatherings
on Sunday are an opportunity to bring together all we have been about during the
week and a time to celebrate our unity in the Lord. The ministries listed under Liturgical Ministries do not require a significant commitment of time but preparation and
dedication are essential.

### LITURGY PREPARATION

01 ___ Liturgy Planning
02 ___ Slide Selection & Filing
03 ___ Eucharistic Bread Baking
04 ___ Banner/Vestment Designer
Sewer and Maker

### LITURGICAL MUSIC

10 ___ Pianist
11 ___ Other Musician
12 ___ Song Leader
13 ___ Choir (Christmas/Easter)

### LITURGICAL MINISTERS

05 ___ Greeter/Usher
06 ___ Eucharistic Minister
07 ___ Lector
08 ___ Slide Operators (age 13 and up)
09 ___ Altar Servers (age 9 and up)

### LITURGICAL DRAMA

14 ___ Actor
15 ___ Drama Reader

## EMMAUS II PROGRAM

Emmaus II is the parish religious education and formation ministry. The Emmaus II
Office is responsible for all educational programs in the parish. The formation of this
parish requires a significant commitment on the part of the community as the following
ministries indicate. To sponsor or serve as a catechist or leader involves a significant
time commitment and a willingness to continue one's personal growth.

### ADULT FORMATION

16 ___ RCIA Sponsor
17 ___ Adult Confirmation Sponsor
18 ___ Adult Formation Committee

### YOUNG PEOPLE'S FAITH FORMATION (GRADES 1–6)

21 ___ Co-Leader
22 ___ Aides
23 ___ Wednesday A.M. Setup

### YOUNG ADULT FAITH FORMATION (GRADES 7–12)

19 ___ Young Adult Conf. Sponsor
20 ___ Conf. Stage 1
Catechist (7th-10th Grade)
20A ___ YOA (Planners & Chaperones)

### YOUNG PEOPLE'S LITURGY OF THE WORD

24 ___ Leader      25 ___ Planner
26 ___ Aide
27 ___ Sunday Liturgy Assistant
28 ___ Baby-sitter — Wed. A.M.
(once a month)

## SOCIAL MINISTRY

Social Ministry encompasses our efforts to serve the wider community and respond to those who are in need. As a parish we make a number of significant commitments premised upon the active participation by parishioners as listed below.

### DIRECT SERVICES

29 ___ Ministry to the sick
30 ___ Funeral Ministry
31 ___ Ministry to the Homeless
32 ___ Soup Kitchen
33 ___ Meals on Wheels
34 ___ Clothing Closet
35 ___ Holmes Convalescent Home
36 ___ AIDS Ministry

### PARISH PROJECTS

37 ___ World Food Day
38 ___ Thanksgiving and Christmas
        Food Baskets
39 ___ Giving Tree (December)

### OFFICE ASSISTANCE

40 ___ Parish Food Pantry
        (weekly/monthly)

## FINANCE MINISTRY

Parish finances are essential if we are to meet the funding requirements for all our ministerial needs. This ministry includes ongoing and single-event opportunities each with their own respective time and staffing requirements.

### ONGOING EFFORTS

41 ___ Ways and Means
42 ___ Bingo Snack Bar Worker
43 ___ Bingo Floor Worker
44 ___ Count & Bank Collections

### MAJOR FUND RAISERS

45 ___ Christmas Bazaar (Nov.)
46 ___ Festival   47 ___ Auction (June)

### FUND RAISERS

48 ___ Bake Sale (Bakers)
49 ___ Crab Feast (August)
50 ___ Spaghetti Dinner (September)
51 ___ All Dances
52 ___ Oyster Roast (October)
53 ___ Ticket Sellers
        (in church–all events)
54 ___ International Dinner (Spring)

## COMMUNITY BUILDERS

Community builders are opportunities to gather the parish so that we might enjoy each other's company. There is no agenda, just food and fun, and the cost is negligible.

55 ___ Summer Picnic
56 ___ Golf Tournament
57 ___ Christmas Decorating
58 ___ New Year's Eve Party

59 ___ Super Bowl Party
60 ___ Cooks (Journeymen or
        Neophytes)
61 ___ Party Setup
62 ___ Party Cleanup

## COMMUNITY SERVICES

### OFFICE ASSISTANCE

63 ___ Art/Work Publicity
64 ___ Office Volunteer

### COMMUNITY SERVICES

65 ___ Bulletin Board
66 ___ Registration Desk
67 ___ Coffee Bar
68 ___ Book Store

## BUILDING AND GROUNDS

69 ___ Plant Care
70 ___ Grounds Care
71 ___ Ascension Construction Crew

72 ___ Carpentry
73 ___ Electrical
74 ___ Plumbing

## HAVE YOU OBTAINED YOUR NAMETAG?

This simple order form is included in this information packet to assist you in obtaining your Ascension nametag. From the beginnings of this community, the use of nametags has been strongly encouraged to facilitate community and extend hospitality. The blue-and-while nametag is used by Ascension parishioners, while neighboring parishes use other colors.

To order nametags, simply put your names as you would like them to appear on the line below and enclose $2.50 for each nametag. This form can be placed in the collection basket or left at the nametag table in the Commons. Your nametags should be available in the Commons within two weeks.

| | |
|---|---|
| NAME | NAME |
| NAME | NAME |
| NAME | NAME |
| NAME | NAME |

NUMBER OF NAMETAGS _____ x $2.50 = $_____
                                    Enclosed Amount

# CHAPTER TWELVE

# St. Ephrem's,
# Sterling Heights, Mich.;
# Mother of Sorrows, Tucson:
# Excellence in Reconciling
# with Hurt, Inactive Members

Father Bob Blondell is a priest in the archdiocese of Detroit. He is one of those people many describe as a pastor-theologian. He is a wonderfully pastoral, people-oriented man. But his ministry is also firmly grounded in sound theology. It was Bob's experience in the late 1970s and 1980s that many of the people coming to the catechumenate were not those seeking baptism or full initiation into the church. They were rather people expressing some hurt or anger against the church, but now apparently feeling a call or pull back to the church. His pastoral sense was that mixing the inactive-now-returning with those joining the church was not good, that the former were a distraction, an undertow for the latter. His theologian side led him to in-depth research into what the ancient church did with the so-called *lapsi*, or lapsed.

Blondell's prayer and study led him to the theological conviction, in accord with St. Paul and others, that the life, death, and resurrection of Jesus has reconciled the world with the Father. He studied the origins of the early catechumenate structure in the second century. The catechumenal process, with importance given to sponsoring, became a generally accepted way of bringing people into the church by the third century. A central pastoral problem of that day was what to do with those who had turned their back on the church or Christ through heresy, murder, or apostasy (denying one's faith). Many were of the opinion that those who had sinned against the vows of their baptism were "out!" Others, like St. Cyprian, were sensitive to the plight of the alienated, and they popularized a process that has come to be known as the Order of Penitents.

The Order of Penitents ran parallel to the catechumenate. People were brought back the way they first entered the church through a process, with multiple rituals, sponsoring, and sharing with the candidates the Word and the Tradition of the church. In his wonderful book *The Reconciling Community*, James Dallen describes how the style of each process, the rituals, and the timing of the words of forgiveness varied from community to community and from East to West.

There seem to have been some common characteristics of the process:

1. There were stages. The *weeper* could stand outside the church in sackcloth and ashes, begging the Lord and the community for mercy. The *kneeler* was allowed inside the church, through he or she had to kneel in the back and was dismissed at the appropriate time. The *stander* was allowed closer to the altar, but in a position of deference to the rest of the congregation. Penitents were dismissed before the Liturgy of the Eucharist began. In most places the process was completed on Holy Thursday, when the bishop welcomed the penitents back to the eucharistic table.

2. For those returning to the Table and those companioning or sponsoring them, prayer, fasting, and almsgiving were emphasized.

3. Companioning or sponsoring were crucial for discerning conversion, repentance, and readiness to return.

4. Not only admission of sin, but confession — profession of God's mercy, love, and forgiveness — was central to the process.

5. Though the process could last as long as three years, Lent, the time of preparation for celebrating the paschal mystery, became a kind of community retreat for the faithful, the catechumens, and the penitents.

6. Holy Thursday became the central day of celebrating God's mercy and the penitents' return to the Table. The bishop would say the words of forgiveness, "May God forgive you..." (as compared to today's "I [the priest] absolve you..."). The bishop would also wash the penitent's feet.

7. The faithful became involved in the life of the penitents, themselves taking on some of their penitential practices of prayer, fasting, and almsgiving.

8. The sign of those seriously engaged in the process of penance was the acceptance of ashes, a sign as trivialized today as the palms on Palm Sunday.

As the Order of Penitents gradually evolved into canonical penance, heavily legalized and juridical, the communal emphasis on both sin and reconciliation began to fade. Privatized sin and reconciliation with exceedingly harsh penances became more normative. In many areas, the sacrament fell into disuse.

Blondell has tried to capture some of the beauty of the ancient Order of Penitents in his "Re-Membering Church" ministry at St. Ephrem's. Though this ministry is targeted on the "alienated," the entire community is invited into the Ash Wednesday to Holy Thursday journey of penance and reconversion. All can be penitents who want to, not only those in the "Re-Membering Church" process.

At St. Ephrem's penance is an espoused *value*, evoking in the community a desire to change. It is a value throughout the year, but especially during the season of Lent. It is experienced also as *process* — prayer, fasting, and almsgiving over many days or weeks, however long it takes. It involves the *naming* of an area of one's life where there is need for healing, forgiveness, and liberation.

While invitation back to the parish happens throughout the year, a special liturgical plateau is the first Sunday of Advent, when those who are intent on staying in the "Re-Membering" community, moving toward Ash Wednesday, are given a wooden cross. The "Re-Membering" community, who will become "the penitents" on Ash Wednesday, are asked to wear the crosses publicly, as a sign to the rest of the community of the importance of penance and the reality of God's healing and forgiving love. Meetings are held weekly, with sessions that focus on the returnees' hurts or questions. Storytelling is encouraged. Scripture is shared, including stories of Jesus' healing, liberating, and forgiving. Throughout, rituals and prayers for healing, liberation, and forgiveness take place. Special emphasis is given to time alone with the returnee's companion or sponsor.

On Ash Wednesday, the entire parish is invited to the Order of Penitents. The ashes are accepted only after one names an area of life in need of God's healing, forgiveness, and liberation and professes that a power greater than hurt, sin, or entrapment can provide rebirth. For many, of course, the taking of ashes is the same traditional annual event, but for others it is a true entrance into the Order of Penitents.

Priests are in church all day on Ash Wednesday at St. Ephrem's for confession and absolution. Or absolution can be deferred to a later time, for example, a communal penance service or Holy Thursday's penitential rite. Each Sunday both catechumens and returning penitents process in with the celebrant and are dismissed after the Liturgy of the Word. Holy Thursday is a ritualization of the return to the Table. At that time, ashes, are washed from the penitents' foreheads by ministers. All who have seriously engaged in the Order of Penitents, including the returnees, are invited to reverence the altar. The returnees continue to celebrate the Triduum with the rest of the penitents and faithful. After Easter, a mystagogical period follows for returning penitents, leading up to Pentecost. After six weeks of prayerful reflection the returning penitents who feel comfortable doing so thank the entire congregation at a Sunday Eucharist for the help and support provided during their journey back to the Table. They also announce to the congregation the ministry they have chosen as active members of the parish community. Blondell and others have found that the best people to minister in the re-membering process are former inactive Catholics.

Blondell feels that the best evangelization for this process is done by people who attend regularly. Neighbors inviting neighbors, family members inviting family members, workers inviting co-workers have been key strategies for evangelization. The community taking ownership of evangelization is a much healthier dynamic than having a few people on an evangelization team.

Those of us who now propagate various versions of a process of reconciliation share with learners the parallels as shown in the accompanying listing.

Not all parishes have been able to implement the Order of Penitents and the "Re-Membering" Church program as well as Bob

# RE-MEMBERING & RCIA: PARALLEL JOURNEY

| RITE OF RE-MEMBERING CHURCH | RITE OF CHRISTIAN INITIATION |
|---|---|

**Welcome**
Time for evangelization through personal stories of pain (often regarding the church) and joy in dialogue with the gospel; questioning and searching for meaning, leading to openness to possible return to the Catholic Church.

**Precatechumenate**
Time for evangelization through personal stories of pain and joy in dialogue with the gospel stories; questioning and searching for meaning, leading to desire to follow Jesus in the Catholic Church.

**Rite of Welcome Back to Community**
Probably in a small group since the person is not sure about return.

**Rite of Acceptance into the Catechumenate**
Normally at a Sunday Eucharist.

**Re-Membering Community**
Time for catechesis in a supportive community of faith, which explores especially in Scripture our tradition of reconciliation offering forgiveness, healing, and liberation; also a time to explore issues and problems that separated the person from the church.

**Catechumenate Community**
Time for catechesis that deepens union with Jesus through sharing faith and witness to mission in a small community and connecting personal stories especially to the tradition of stories in the Sunday lectionary.

**Rite of Re-Membering**
First stage of the sacrament of reconciliation with a public ritual (possibly with ashes on Ash Wednesday) and private confession.

**Rite of Election**
Celebration of God's call through the church to the Easter sacraments.

**Lenten Illumination and Purification**
A six-week retreat with prayer, penance, and penitential rites that heal, purify, and strengthen.

**Lenten Illumination and Purification**
A six-week retreat with Scripture reflection, prayer, spiritual direction, liturgies of the Scrutinies, which purify and strengthen.

**Completion of the Sacrament of Reconciliation**
Absolution, perhaps on Wednesday of Holy week, or at a penitential rite during Holy Thursday's Mass of the Lord's Supper; reception of Eucharist on Holy Thursday.

**Sacrament of Initiation**
Celebration of baptism, confirmation, Eucharist at the Easter Vigil.

**Mystagogia**
Time to celebrate the journey, especially at Sunday Eucharist, and to prepare for commitment to mission on Pentecost, supported by a small group and sponsor.

**Mystagogia**
Time to celebrate the journey, especially at Sunday Eucharist, and to prepare for commitment to mission on Pentecost, supported by a small group and sponsor.

Blondell has. Theologian-pastor and author Robert Duggan has raised questions about whether the Rite of Penance is the most honest ritual with which to address the many types of hurt and healing and to celebrate the reconciliation that came through a re-membering process. Father Duggan says that for some anointing or the laying on of hands may be more appropriate.

Another model of a process of return — similar to the Church of the Holy Spirit's "Once a Catholic..." — is Alienated Catholics Anonymous (ACA), a process pioneered by Msgr. Thomas Cahalane. Msgr. Cahalane was born in Glendare in County Cork, studied at St. Patrick's Seminary in Carlow, Ireland, and was ordained in 1963 for the diocese of Tucson. For years, Tom was the vicar of education and now is the director of ecumenical and inter-religious affairs for the diocese.

Alienated Catholics Anonymous is a series of informal pastoral sessions that attempt to create an environment of invitation and welcome for Catholics who have "been away." Cahalane targets the peak times of Christmas and Easter, using the usually overcrowded Masses to extend an invitation to those who have been away to participate in a session held after Christmas and after Easter. Cahalane began tinkering with the idea of working with the alienated in 1985. He confesses to borrowing the title from another pastoral experience whose story was told in a magazine. In a true spirit of model innovation, Cahalane and Mother of Sorrows devised a process that seems to fit their local pastoral setting. Cahalane finds that many of the inactive whom he has worked with have been interested in returning to the church but have not known where or how to start. Some have been rebuffed in some way by a church representative or and have not had the personal contact needed to untangle divorce–remarriage–annulment situations.

Like "Once a Catholic..." the process consists of six sessions, offered twice a year; participants often express a desire that the process go longer. Cahalane has been criticized for being input-oriented, but perhaps we forget how basic some potential returnees' questions or problems can be.

In the first session, Cahalane shares a profile of his own life and then asks the people to do the same, at least anonymously by answering a few basic questions. That way he has a better feel for "where the people are coming from." The profile questions, in the form of sentence completions, are:

1.  I am here because:

2.  My hopes/expectations in being here are:

3.  My fears/apprehensions in being here are:

4.  My feelings about the church at this time are:

5.  My feelings about God at this time are:

6.  The questions/issues I most want answered in these sessions are:

    Other Comments:

...

Cahalane conducts the sessions with teams made up of former ACA groups. From the first sessions he tries to create a mood and agenda of reconciliation. At the first session he highlights that the sacrament of reconciliation is a celebration of "coming home." At the second session he spends time on forgiveness and reconciliation. Notice that in good andragogical fashion, the returnees' questions were solicited in the initial profile. These are dealt with throughout the process. The third session focuses on human sexuality, marriage, divorce, remarriage, and annulment. The fourth session is on "Our God as a Table God," with most of the time given to Eucharist. Other Catholic devotions and practices are highlighted. The fifth session is a catch-all on Catholic practices, but also moves into the area of baptismal spirituality and ministry. Members of various ministries explain what they do and how they function in the parish. An invitation is extended to consider one's own gifts and possible involvement. At the fifth session, it is explained that the final session will be a special teaching Mass, at which those who have been away from the Eucharist are welcome to share in communion. Encouragement is extended to celebrate reconciliation before the sixth session. At the sixth session, at which the various parts of the Mass are explained and Eucharist is shared by those who feel called, there is a follow-up dinner celebration called the Prodigal Son's and Daughter's Banquet.

Publicity for the post-Christmas series starts in early December, alerting parishioners, who are encouraged to invite possible returnees, and extending the invitation via extraparochial means. Publicity for the post-Easter series begins in mid-February. Publicity includes pulpit announcements, plus an occasional brief presentation by someone who has returned via ACA. Here is a paraphrase of a recent one given at a Christmas Mass.

> I am _____, a graduate of Alienated Catholics Anonymous. I have recently returned to the church. Coming back to church has given my life new meaning and purpose. I found the ACA sessions enriching and helpful in becoming active in my faith again. If you have been away, as I was, I encourage you to get more information about these sessions and to attend. If you know of someone who could benefit from these sessions, please pass the word on to them.

The personal witness value in such an announcement is inestimable.

Consciousness is also raised as the needs of ACA and inactive Catholics in general are placed in the general intercessions of many weekend liturgies. Thus, in many ways the entire parish is gradually immersed in a missionary spirit, if not by active involvement in the Alienated Catholics Anonymous process, then by invitation to pray for the effort.

Andrew Greeley, who cautions us frequently about creating too many legal hurdles for both returning Catholics and those joining the church for the first time, has expressed an endorsement of Cahalane's pastoral wisdom and strategies.

# CHAPTER THIRTEEN

# Old St. Patrick's Parish, Chicago: Excellence in Young Adult Ministry

Sixteen thousand young adults from their early twenties to mid-forties received an invitation recently to celebrate Sunday Eucharist in parishes in the archdiocese of Chicago. One such parish is Old St. Patrick's, the archdiocese's oldest church. A survivor of the Chicago fire, several years ago St. Patrick's had only a few parishioners because the parish was located on Skid Row, not far from the hotel where the infamous Richard Speck hid from police after murdering several young nurses.

Someone asked me some years ago why I did not consider applying for the pastorate of St. Patrick's when it became available. My first response was, "Why in the name of God would someone want St. Patrick's?" My question was based on its history at the time. It had become a place for lunch-time Mass for the very devoted. People from the west end of Chicago's downtown could quickly walk over to St. Pat's on a nice day. But after working hours, the sidewalks were rolled up. The only ones who roamed the streets were the alcoholics, the addicts, the homeless, and the prostitutes.

Father Jack Wall knew more about the changing demographics of Chicago than I when he consented to be St. Patrick's pastor in the mid-1980s. The city had already begun the construction of huge residential dwellings called Presidential Towers; old printing houses were being gutted and turned into apartments and lofts; trendy businesses were popping up where the poorest of the poor used to sleep on the sidewalks. Chicago's Near West Side was being gentrified, and in the process thousands of young people raised in the suburbs and others transplanted from other areas were moving into the neighborhood.

The young adults, like those mentioned in the chapter on mega-churches, seemed different from those of years past — looking for something, searching spiritually. Often spiritually rootless after being away from church for years, they began to find some roots, paradox-ically in a gaudy old church, with poor architecture and art, from another historical setting. They seemed to find roots also in the city, with its economic attraction of new jobs. They seemed to find in St. Patrick's, and a few other churches, an alternative to the bars and other gathering places that they had tried and found wanting.

It was not by default that St. Patrick's has become a magnet church for young adults. Pastor Jack Wall is a pastoral innovator and en-trepreneur. He asked Father John Cusick, director of Chicago's Young Adult Ministry office, to be resident-associate. John is a passionate preacher and liturgist. So is Father Dan Cantwell, now retired, but a grandfather figure of great wisdom who was conducting catechume-nal processes for the unchurched in the 1960s long before the rite was promulgated. Also hired was John Fontana, nationally known for his work in youth ministry. John has taken a different turn in directing the Crossroad Center, an organization devoted to helping adults of all ages to connect their faith with the workplace.

Over the years the staff has given great care to hiring people for liturgy and music, realizing that worship is frequently the most im-portant evangelizing moment for young adults. They also have hired people skilled in the ministries of the catechumenate for the many who want to join the church as well as for the many already baptized in need of the other sacraments of initiation.

St. Patrick's has followed the pattern of Willowcreek, though anchored firmly in the Catholic tradition. Through effective wor-ship and needs-oriented programs, it first attracted young adults. The young adults have convinced their mid-life and older parents of St. Patrick's uniqueness. Weekend worship is now bursting at the seams, largely with young adults, but also with a healthy inter-generational mixture. St. Patrick's does not fit the canonically de-termined territorial parish definition. People came from all over the metropolitan area for worship and ministries at St. Patrick's.

Hospitality and welcome are hallmarks of St. Patrick's. A form in each weekend's bulletin invites people to take initial steps for regis-tration in the parish. The hall beneath the church is frequently used after Sunday Masses for coffee, rolls, and discussion of the readings and the homily. Christmas and Easter are celebrated in grand style, recalling the best of Catholic tradition as well as some of the nostalgia like that evoked by a 1940s movie about those special days.

Jack Wall is politically astute and media wise. The city's traditional St. Patrick's Day parade begins with Mass at the church. The Mass is standing-room only, with worshippers out on the church steps. During the summer the parish sponsors a fund-raiser entitled "The World's Largest Block Party." Using an entire square block, the parish attracts national musical acts and many local restaurants and media personalities to a summer Mardi Gras. All of this needs to be seen as healthy "marketing" of the parish, as effective evangelization. Significant attempts have been made to visit people in their homes in the towering condos and other residential facilities that now abound in the area. Reach-out, then, is both local and city-wide.

When it comes to adult faith formation, St. Patrick's staff realizes that many who would attend evening sessions have a commute awaiting them to another part of the city or the suburbs. Therefore, unlike many parishes that hold adult education at 7:30 or 8:00 P.M., they target the dinner hour. The educational program is joined to a simple meal of soup and salad. The gathering disperses at 7:30 or 8:00 P.M. to leave for home. Days of quite practical retreat, are held, like an upcoming one entitled "Transitions: A Day to Explore Movements in Your Work Life," cosponsored by the Young Adult Ministry Office. The latter office in cooperation with St. Pat's also offers Adult Children of Alcoholics meetings as well as divorced and separated groups for young adults. In most parishes these very helpful support groups are more oriented toward mid-lifers than to divorced and separated young people.

On the first Sunday of every month a Mass especially dedicated to the needs, concerns, and worship style of young adults is held at 11:15 A.M., followed by a continental breakfast. Father Dave Murphy, another staff member, regularly advertises in the bulletin that he will meet alone or in a group with inactive, recovering, or disenchanted Catholics.

The extended staff of St. Patrick's reveals some of the parish's unique directions: president of community outreach; coordinator of the shelter program; coordinators of adult literacy; nursery during Mass coordinators; new members' dinner coordinator; stewardship chairperson; director of communications; business manager.

The first new school to open in the archdiocese of Chicago in recent years ironically opened at Chicago's oldest church, St. Patrick's. With some nearby residents seeking trustworthy day care, kindergarten, and first grade, St. Patrick's has cautiously begun a parochial school. Its old school was rented out years ago during the parish's lean years; the convent has been given to the Crossroads Center and other ministries. Thus St. Patrick's school is a "pilgrim school" or a "school without walls," renting space at a nearby high-rise condo development.

———

The impact of St. Patrick's along with the pioneering work of Father John Cusick and Kate DeVries in Young Adult Ministry and John Fontana have sparked other parishes in the archdiocese to make young adults a deliberate concern. Among them are Ascension parish in Oak Park, Our Lady of Perpetual Help in Glenview, Holy Family in Inverness, Our Lady of Mount Carmel in Chicago, St. Edna's in Arlington Heights, St. Michael's in Orland Park, and several regional efforts like Lake County Young Adults and Southeast Suburban Young Adults — all in the archdiocese of Chicago.

Several other parishes in the center city are being gentrified or yuppified. Among them are St. Michael's on Cleveland Avenue in Chicago and St. Clement's in the beautiful Lincoln Park area. At St. Clement's, according to journalist (and parishioner) Tim Unsworth, young adults age 18–35 come to the Eucharist more often than those in the 35 to 54 age range. According to Tim, 75 percent of St. Clement's population are young females, 83 percent of whom are college graduates. Fifty-six percent of the parishioners are married. More than half earn $60,000 or more a year. St. Michael's and St. Clement's have also had to develop the effective worship and needs-based programs and ministries modeled so well by St. Patrick's.

The average age of a typical Catholic churchgoer in Chicago is 47. Unless more parishes learn from parishes like St. Patrick's, the church in the United States runs the risk of experiencing the European phenomenon of the "graying of the church." Thousands of young adults are distant from their parish communities, because nothing is being done for them — or allowed to be done by them.

In a stirring address to CORPUS (Corps of Reserve Priests United for Service), *Commonweal* magazine editor Margaret Steinfels O'Brien lamented the politics of confrontation between liberal and conservative Catholics while a serious malaise exists under our ideological noses:

> Is there anyone confident that the faith has been successfully passed on to the next generation? Does anyone believe that the postconciliar period has produced a religious renewal among young people? We await the return of the baby-boomer.... We focus our gaze on the small number of admirable young people...who we instinctively feel have "caught the church...." But what about the far greater number who are passing into adulthood and career with a very meager store of Catholicism's theological and spiritual riches?...They often lack the most elementary habits of prayer or understanding of the sacraments.

In the light of her words, thank God for the mission statement of Old St. Patrick's:

> The mission of Old St. Patrick's Church is to serve life and the work of the laity in the world. Standing steadfast at the cross-road of a historic past and a promising future, in the midst of the rich diversity of Chicago, we are convinced that the mystery of Jesus Christ's life, death, and resurrection unfolds within human life. Therefore we resolve:
>
> - to probe the meaning of our adult experiences of work, relationships, and family, that, guided by the Holy Spirit, we might ground our faith in our secular vocations and responsibilities;
>
> - to create and sustain a community of hospitality and friendship, of prayer and service, that we might celebrate the goodness of life and respond to human needs;
>
> - to commit ourselves to embodying and promoting the values and actions that arise from our common reflection, that we might influence our society in positive ways.

As members and staff of Old St. Patrick's, we embrace these tasks as a continuation of the mission of Jesus Christ, so that others may experience, in freedom, the rich promise of God's love for our world.

# CHAPTER FOURTEEN

# St. Michael's Parish, Orland Park, Ill.: Excellence in Parish Governance

St. Michael's used to be a little white frame church in a rural area southwest of Chicago. Now it is the "cathedral" of the southwest suburbs, spawning four new parishes in the last fifteen years and still with over four thousand families registered. A recurring theme of this book is that excellent parishes have structures that fit their mission. St. Michael's has become a beacon for many parishes around the country in developing a truly effective governance body, technically called the PMC, or Parish Ministry Commission. Central to St. Michael's evolving mission is an awareness of all the baptized as gifted and called to mission and ministry. The PMC was designed to animate and facilitate that mission.

St. Michael's has taken the time and effort to develop a spirituality and theology of giftedness. Key to the vision is that gifts or charisms are to be shared — for the common good, to the glory of God. In theologizing about gifts, the parish made a distinction between gifts and talents. Talents usually are employed for self-aggrandizement, but charisms are always to be shared *for* others and *for* God. A talent can became a gift or charism. Among the many gifts that St. Michael's has focused on are:

- faith
- energy
- potential
- growth
- willingness
- hope

- freedom
- talents
- strengths
- weaknesses
- resources
- one's own life

101

The harnessing/unleashing of giftedness is accomplished through the activity of the Parish Ministry Commission, working closely with the parish staff and the pastor. St. Michael's uses the accompanying diagram to visualize the life and activity of the parish.

Circle one, the innermost circle, represents the position of the pastor. The pastor works with the professional staff and the Parish Ministry Commission. Circle two represents the parish staff. These people have been appointed or employed for their special capabilities and include priests, sisters, transitional and permanent deacons, and laity with specific professional abilities. Some of the staff represent the five ministry areas or teams. These five staff members also become part of the PMC. The third circle represents the PMC, composed of the pastor, the five staff members, lay members from the ministry teams, and lay members appointed by the pastor. The PMC provides direction for the parish and sets specific goals in congruence with the mission statement. The fourth circle represents the five main ministry teams: worship, parish life, service, education, and youth. The ministry teams are comprised of staff members and pastoral lay leaders (PLLs) who coordinate and work with the lay leaders involved in direct ministries with each of the five ministry areas. Circle five represents the pastoral lay leaders. Their interest, responsibility and commitment are bidirectional. They focus on the last circle — direct ministry — as well as ministry teams (circle four) that oversee their particular areas of ministry. The PLLs work with the parish activity lay leaders to implement the parish goals. The sixth circle represents all the activities of the parish's direct ministries. Each ministry is headed by its own Lay leader. This is the most important level of activity and ministry, at the grassroots level. Without this level, there is no reason

---

### MISSION STATEMENT OF ST. MICHAEL'S CHURCH

Each of you received a special gift. Use it, in service to one another.                                                    — 1 Peter 4:10

The faith community of St. Michael's is called by the Father, gifted by the Son, and moved by the Spirit to unite in witnessing to the gospel message. We celebrate, proclaim, share in friendship, and serve as a parish committed to ministering to the needs of all God's people.

## ST. MICHAEL'S ORGANIZATIONAL CHART

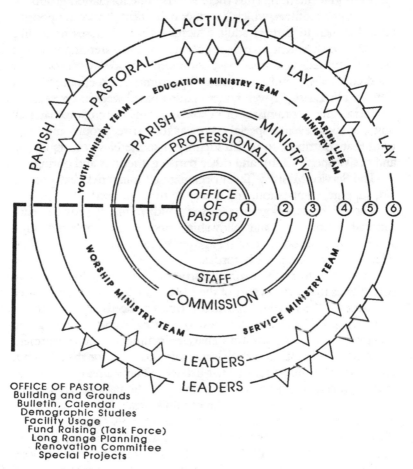

OFFICE OF PASTOR
Building and Grounds
Bulletin, Calendar
Demographic Studies
Facility Usage
Fund Raising (Task Force)
Long Range Planning
Renovation Committee
Special Projects

for the superstructure, the roles created by the structure, or the vision contained in the parish mission statement.

The Worship Ministry Team not only coordinates all the various ministries involved in weekend worship, but also strives to educate and form the congregation in sound liturgical theory and behavior, emphasizing the ministry of the assembly.

The Education Team coordinates, supports, and encourages a total religious education program and all direct ministries involved in it. Special attention is given to opportunities for adult religious ed-

ucation and formation. Thus there is a daytime formation group for
stay-at-home mothers, which provides baby-sitting; special opportunities for men to gather; adult education that addresses needs like
grief and bereavement; marriage enrichment and parenting training;
"Parish Spirituality," a small base community process with over four
hundred involved; and an ongoing opportunity to experience "Christ
Renews His Parish," a well-known parish-based weekend retreat.

Parish Life is a ministry of hospitality. This team coordinates all
ongoing social events, special events as they arise, groups and functions that contribute to parish identity (like the Newcomers Group
and the Women's Club), and other parish gatherings and outings.

The Service Ministry Team organizes all ministries that provide
aid, support, compassion, and mercy to those in need.

The newest addition, a team for youth ministry, provides educational, formational, and fellowship opportunities for junior high
students, high schoolers, college-age people, and young adults in their
twenties, thirties, and early forties.

In addition to the five main ministry teams, there are four standing
committees that serve as part of the PMC. The formation committee
provides for the ongoing spiritual formation needs of PMC members. The governance and by-laws committee oversees the ongoing
updating of the organization's charter document. The recruitment
committee, attempts to surface leadership, not only for the PMC but
all the various ministries of St. Michael's. The training committee
shapes, offers, and evaluates the training of the pastoral lay leaders,
and also the lay leaders of the direct ministries.

Two members from each ministry team are also members of the
PMC. One staff member from each of the areas of ministry is on the
PMC. Vacancies on the PMC are filled by a gradual, prayerful process
of discernment. Lay members serve for an initial two-year term. They
can serve one or two additional one-year terms. Three lay members
can be appointed by the pastor for one-year terms. Staff members
serve for one-year terms. By office, the pastor is a permanent member.

To become a member of the PMC, one has to be experienced
in ministry. Potential members most have completed thirty hours of
St. Michael's pastoral lay leadership classes and a minimum of one
year of service to the parish as a pastoral lay leader.

Nowhere have I seen the Order of Initiation or the catechumenate
implemented better than at St. Michael's. Rather than the fall-to-
spring linear model, which prevails in so many parishes, St. Michael's

"Enter the Living Waters" process is better represented by a circle. At least four times a year there is a Ritual of Acceptance, launching another group on the journey toward initiation. It is a messy process deciding when groups should be spliced together, discerning who is ready for Easter sacraments, and dismissing candidates from Mass to "break open the Word" after the Liturgy of the Word — year round! It is messy, but healthy in its chaos, and a process that facilitates genuine conversion much more than linear program models, which often are simply instruction *classes* with a few scrutinies and exorcisms thrown in.

What strikes me most about St. Michael's parish is its genuine commitment — in the Parish Ministry Commission and in other aspects of parish life — to discernment. In example after example, teams, committees, and groups prayerfully more toward consensus in decision making. People genuinely wait on God for truth to emerge. I sat through several discernment sessions at St. Michael's — and found them gruelling. The pragmatist in me wanted to rush to a more expedient solution to an issue, decision, or choice of a person. I can see, however, how much more valuable relying on the process of waiting on the Holy Spirit is.

I sense St. Michael's is at a crossroads, however. The Parish Ministry Commission coordinates the many ministries and programs of the parish. But Father Ed McLaughlin, appointed pastor several years ago, is also interested in issues discussed in other chapters, like neighborhood ministers and small Christian communities, even beyond what the "Parish Spirituality" programs accomplishes. How these emerging relational efforts will alter and be subsumed by the PMC remains to be seen.

# CHAPTER FIFTEEN

# St. John the Evangelist Parish, Streamwood, Ill.: Excellence in Family Consciousness

---

The U.S. bishops' pastoral *A Family Perspective in Church and Society* (1987) called for an end to "the farming out" of family functions to "the professionals." The bishops recognized the diversity of family typology, defining family as, an intimate community of persons bonded by blood, marriage, or adoption (or choice), serving life, serving as a community for social training, in dialogue with God, sharing in the mission of the church.

Bishop Michael Pfeiffer, bishop of San Angelo, Texas, issued a wonderful pastoral letter on February 12, 1988, entitled *The Family and the Kingdom of God*. In it he describes the family as the primary place where children and parents experience the values and behaviors that epitomize the Kingdom of God preached by Jesus. The family, the domestic church, is, or ought to be, the first experience of community. Admitting the brokenness found in many marriages and families, Pfeiffer nonetheless speaks of the family's potential to be the first, best place to appropriate Christ's values and behaviors; the first, best experience of learning how to use both time and money; the first, best experience of learning the importance of service and ministry and respect for life in all its forms. Basic spiritual skills like prayer and worship are best learned in the family.

One parish where I have worked as a consultant is St. John's in Streamwood, Illinois. St. John's has made a tremendous commitment to family consciousness, or family perspective, despite restrictions of budget and meeting space.

After studying Ascension parish in Virginia Beach, St. John's also decided to use "Emmaus" as a title that encompasses all its religious education efforts. Compartmentalized, splintered efforts, like parochial school and religious education programs (CCD), were reimagined as two expressions of one united effort. Both of these, as well as sacramental catechesis (preparation), were put on a family-based model. Also under the "Emmaus" umbrella are the Order of Initiation, adult education ("Beacon"), the "Remember and Return" process for alienated Catholics, and several other processes evangelical and catechetical in nature.

The language of boards, teams, and councils has been dropped and replaced with *community:* the Emmaus community, the Worship community, the Caring Hearts community, the Administration community, and the Parish Leadership community, which coordinates the ministries of the other communities. This was not just a jargon change. All leaders serving on those organizations are to set an example for the rest of the community by engaging regularly in four steps constitutive of small Christian communities: praying together; reading Scripture; sharing life; and ministering. Notice they are not to jump into the tasks of ministry. Ministry is to be rooted in richer soil — the other three elements. Father Bill Moriarity, the pastor, summed up the vision in a recent bulletin article, which we include on the following page.

St. John's staff — Father Bill Moriarity, pastor, Father Bill Burke and Sister Kathleen LaPlume, associate pastors, and several in recent years who have served in the various roles of school administrator, religious education coordinator, and youth minister — have used one of the weekend liturgies for a family-oriented Mass. Parishioners have been educated in this family emphasis and are able to choose whether to share in such a liturgy or go to another one. The process has evolved to the point that school and religious education families work together with Sr. Kathleen in planning and ministering the family Masses. Usually the 9:30 A.M. Mass on Sunday is for primary and intermediate grades. One week primary grades are the focus; the next week, there is an intermediate focus. Junior high family Masses are usually celebrated at the 5:30 Saturday evening liturgy of anticipation. Often, especially with the younger children, the Sunday readings are taken from a children's Bible,

## A WORD WITH YOU ...
### by Father Bill Moriarity

*Last February, Cardinal Bernardin directed pastors and parish staffs throughout the archdiocese to begin to develop a networking system in which parishioners, organizations, and staff could be linked together in the call to follow the Lord.*

*Listed below is a design that has been worked on by the extended staff. The design attempts to show a networking movement of people united in baptism of faith in Christ. A parish mission statement shapes the direction of pastoral efforts.*

*The parish leadership community is what was once known as the parish council. Its purpose is to assist me or any pastor in planning how the call of Jesus can take effect in this area of God's Reign. Some of the leadership community's concerns are the development of the spiritual and pastoral goals as well as to do long-range planning and visioning for the parish. In networking the staff, parish organizations, and parish membership, the hope is that pastoring to the community will be inclusive and effective.*

*At this time extended staff members are discerning the names of people from the four umbrella communities. It is my hope to have membership for this leadership community. As you can see this design is a call for all of us to be involved in the pastoring call of Jesus.*

especially if the lectionary version is difficult for young people to understand. Often even the adults seem to appreciate the simpler version. Drama, readers' theater style presentations, recorded music, slides, and other techniques are used to enhance the proclamation of the Word.

Not only at official family Masses, but at every weekend liturgy, families not only bring up the gifts, but also prepare the table for the Liturgy of the Eucharist.

Family Masses are "packaged" as an essential part of the curriculum of both the parochial school and the religious education program. While the staff refuses to police attendance, it is obvious that many mothers, fathers, grandparents, and other guardians are bringing their children to Mass and worshipping with them. For a community to reclaim the Eucharist — gathering around the Word and the Table and being sent forth in mission as the central piece of its faith formation process — is a powerful corporate conversion. Families not just children, are being evangelized. Recent studies by Wade Clark Roof and others conclude that often children are the occasion for their parents who have become inactive in church to return to an active practice of the faith. Curiously, in many parishes where a family model is being implemented, parochial school parents seem the most resistant to becoming involved. The attitude almost seems to be "I pay good money not to have to be involved in this." While Bill Moriarity and the staff listen to some criticism and make some adaptations, they stick to their core conviction that family involvement is mandatory.

While the 9:30 A.M. Sunday Mass is going on, other things are happening over in the multipurpose room in the school. On some Sundays families prepare for First Eucharist; on other Sundays other families, preparing for First Reconciliation, gather for family catechesis. The catechesis is spread throughout the year, following the stages of the catechumenate. There is an evangelizing period for awakening or reawakening faith. There is a time for suitable formation, or catechesis. There is a time for proximate preparation. There is the sacramental celebration itself and an admonition that the sacramental moment not be a graduation, but the assuming of a new relationship with Christ and the church. Public rites at Sunday liturgies are sprinkled throughout the year. At the 9:30 A.M. session, a simple breakfast is provided. There is catechesis for adults, and children go elsewhere for catechesis on their level. They gather for a family experience at

- **CARING HEARTS**
- Ministers of Care
  - Hospitals
  - Nursing Homes
  - Shut-Ins
- Senior Citizens
- Food Pantry
- H.U.G.S.
- Hospitality
- Alcoholics Anonymous
- Substance Abuse
- Rainbows/Spectrum
- Hispanic Ministry
- Heart Sisters
- Families Anonymous

- **PRAYER & WORSHIP**
- Liturgy Board
- Liturgy Planning
  - Seasonal Planners
  - Family Mass Planners
  - Jr. High Mass Planners
- Lectors/Eucharistic Ministers
- Art/Environment
- Music Ministers
  - Choir
  - Cantor
  - Instrumentalists
  - Folk Choir
- Ushers/Greeters
- Altar Servers

- **EMMAUS**
- St. John's School
  - Staff
  - School Board
  - P.T.C.
  - Volunteers
- School of Religion
  - Catechists
  - Eucharist
  - Reconciliation
  - Children's Catechumenate
  - Volunteers
- **FLAME**
  - Ministry of Word
  - Special Services
  - Social Events
  - Supportive Services
- Adults/Young Adults
  - Beacon/Little Rock Bible
  - Baptism Preparation
  - Marriage Prep/Prepare
  - RCIA
  - Remember and Return
  - School of Ministry
  - Parish Library

- **ADMINISTRATION**
- Building/Maintenance
- Finance
- Bingo
- Collection Counters
- Registration
- Secretarial Staff
- Reach Out 1991
- Memorials
- Publications

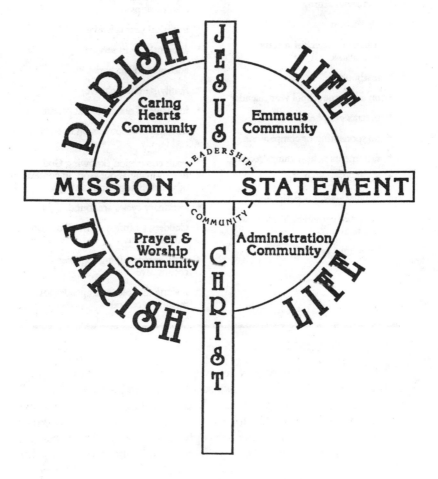

| SCHOOLING | GRADUAL INITIATION |
|---|---|
| • geared to age, ability | • gradual immersion of child and family into community |
| • graded | |
| • classroom setting | • experience of faith-filled relationships |
| • instruction | • liturgical year calendar |
| • teacher or catechist mostly responsible | • apprenticing in service |
| | • anchored in Eucharist |
| • textbooks | • family/parent inclusive |
| • on academic school year calendar | • inclusive of noncustodial parent |
| • parents peripheral | • discerning of conversion in child and family |
| • no sponsoring or companioning | |
| • sacraments as holy things received | • goal: conversion (knowing God, not knowing about God, in context of worshipping community) |
| • graduation mind-set | |
| • Sunday assembly peripheral | • lectionary cycles are foundational |
| • Scripture chosen to fit the flow of a textbook | • Children's Liturgy of the Word on a regular basis |
| • traditional prayers learned | • families worshiping together as constitutive |
| | • making disciples and apostles for mission is central |

about 10:30 A.M., where they are assigned a task to be done together at home relevant to the family's sacramental preparation. Then all go over to the 11:00 A.M. Sunday Eucharist. Again, Eucharist is experienced as central to faith formation and religious education. Here again attendance is not policed, though parochial school teachers and catechists must note who is being irresponsible about preparing for the sacrament.

Through the "Beacon" adult education series, St. John's sponsors events to enrich marriage, family life, and parenting. St. John's also has implemented its own style of the FLAME program, using the consultation of both the Evangelization Office, which I direct, and St. John Neumann parish in St. Charles, Illinois. Parallel to FLAME at St. John's is another process called "Spectrum." It is an ongoing support group for teens who have lost a parent, either through divorce or death. Assistance is given in the grieving and coping process. FLAME and Spectrum complement each other.

St. John's latest addition is Children's Liturgy of the Word. On a monthly basis, at one of the Masses a bell is rung before the first reading, calling primary and intermediate children to the large sacristy for proclamation and sharing on their level. After the homily, the bell is rung again, inviting the children to return to offer praise with their parents during the Liturgy of the Eucharist.

As much as I admire St. John's family perspective, I believe they have only begun to scratch the surface of something of greater profundity than just family perspective, namely, the whole orientation toward how we do religious education. St. John's has begun to experiment with a model of gradual initiation of individuals and families into community to replace a schooling model. As with many other parishes doing this experimentation, St. John's is maintaining the traditional school and religious education classes to insure systematic catechesis, but it has begun to supplement these efforts with other pieces that speak of religious education as a process of initiation into community rather than cerebral knowledge about God and church. There is a marked difference in emphasis between the schooling and initiation models, as shown in the accompanying list.

On a regular basis names of other parishes trying a family-based liturgical process cross my desk:

- St. Francis of Assisi, Centerville, Ohio

- St. Peter's, Waldorf, Maryland

- Presentation, Upper Saddle River, New Jersey

- St. Blase's, Bellingham, Maine

- Our Lady of Sorrows, Fairfax, New Jersey

- St. Edmund's, Manchester, New Hampshire

- Holy Family, Inverness, Illinois

- Many of the parishes in the diocese of Richmond, Virginia

- Church of the Immaculate Conception, Irwin, Pennsylvania

Some excellent resources supportive of the vision expressed in this chapter are:

- *Sundays*, Treehaus Communications
- *Seasons of Faith*, ROA Brown
- *Family-Intergenerational Religious Education*, F.I.R.E. (Kathleen Chesto)
- *Sunday's Story*, Tabor Publishing
- *Living Water*, Tabor Publishing
- *Spirit Magazine*, lectionary-based catechesis for teens

If there is any "sacred cow" that will resist model innovation for excellence, in this case, excellence in catechetical renewal, it is the religious education of children in parochial schools, parish religious education programs, and sacramental catechesis. In no other area of parish life are the words "But we have always done it this way!" used so frequently as an escape hatch from excellence.

# CHAPTER SIXTEEN

# Pastoral Alliances for Excellence: Anywhere, the Future

At an early morning meeting of pastors in Toledo, we focused on the issues they most wanted to talk about. One was children's Liturgy of the Word. One pastor protested that he would never have it — that it did not assure enough systematic catechesis. But several others spoke up saying that they had begun such a supplement to parochial school and CCD and it was working beautifully. The witness and challenge of his two peers did more to convince the doubting pastor at least to open the door on the topic than any words I could have expressed.

On this issue and others, I saw pastors in a peer-to-peer ministry acting as resources for each other and challenging each other to become innovative and excellent in ministry. The Toledo meeting, two days in length, was an annual meeting of the Pastoral Alliance, a network of some fifteen or twenty parishes in the diocese of Toledo. Begun some years ago under the supervision of Dr. Robert Newsome, a clinical psychologist and organizational consultant, these pastors and their staffs are consultants to each other for support, challenge, idea swapping, and what Tom Peters would call model innovation.

After directing a diocesan office for some years now and being the guest speaker at various clerical cluster meetings, I am convinced that "downtown" would operate better if it sought only to serve as a facilitator for clusters of staffs, not just priests, to become consultants to each other in pastoral alliances for excellence. Put another way, I ought to be concerned not only about my own parish, but about the parish next door and the parish across town: I ought to be concerned that we are all excellent parishes! The opposite is competition and congregationalism.

The notion of pastoral alliances for excellence need not apply only to interparish relationships. How much more healthy the church at large would be if the following imagined themselves as pastoral alliances for excellence: individual staffs, parish councils, clusters of parishes, faculties, individual ministry teams, boards, deaneries, vicariates.

In consulting with a large Midwestern archdiocese recently, I began to see that their day-to-day practices "downtown" often mirror the parishes and, more than they would like to admit, the parishes mirror downtown. Specifically, the archdiocese wanted me to facilitate a day around the following issues for both downtown agencies and parish staffs on both the intraparish and interparish levels:

- How can we minister more in a "communion" or "co-laboring" mode rather than being compartmentalized and isolated in our own ministries?

- How can we create more flexible structures that fit our core mission to evangelize and help people with conversion?

- How can we better be consultants to each other, helping each other especially in the burdens of our ministries?

- How can we become less competitive with each other and more concerned with each other's excellence in ministry?

- How can we move from a "maintenance" model of church to one of mission?

As these diocesan leaders wrestled with these issues, it became clear that to achieve the ideals presupposed in the above questions there would have to be conversions: individual conversions of staff members, corporate conversions of staffs, corporate conversions of parishioners, and corporate conversion of the church as a whole.

Father Ted Stone, of Our Lady Mother of the Church parish on Chicago's Northwest Side, coordinates a kind of pastoral alliance for excellence. He has convinced eighteen of twenty-five surrounding parishes of the value of meeting around the various ministries of consolation going on in each of the eighteen parishes. The ministers involved in ministries of healing and compassion simply swap ideas and examples of what is going on in their parishes relative to pastoral care. Ted and others tell stories of how parish "X" got a core idea from parish "Y," took it, enhanced it, and organically developed their own unique approach and style.

What Ted does in pastoral care could be done in all facets of ministry. Networks of parishes, in line with the Toledo model, could gather regularly and swap ideas and models around issues like these:

- What are we doing for and with teens?

- What are effective models for young adult ministry?

- What is working in adult education?

- What are some models of effective family-based religious education?

- What are some models of reaching out to inactive Catholics?

Such model innovation and networking is being coordinated beautifully by Robert Humphrey of the Religious Education Department in the diocese of Manchester, New Hampshire, around the issue of catechetical renewal.

Msgr. Robert Fuller of Tucson, Arizona, summed up the major concern of this book in a recent article on small base communities. He said that despite heroic efforts by staffs and lay volunteers our parishes are not working. They are not working if we maintain that our core goal is conversion. We are not facilitating conversion in people's lives, despite a flurry of busyness and programs. Fuller suggests that it is because we are afraid to think of the parish in new paradigms. He told the now famous story of the Swiss watchmakers who refused to innovate with the newly invented digital battery-powered watch. The idea was picked up, however, by Seiko and the Japanese. The Swiss no longer to make 70 percent of the world's watches. Now the Japanese do.

It is time for dioceses and parishes, stuck in "paradigm paralysis," courageously to risk resources and personnel to create on various levels of ecclesial life pastoral alliances for excellence.

# CHAPTER SEVENTEEN

# Benchmarking Parishes

---

I learned a new term from my friends in the corporate world. It is called *benchmarking*. Between 60 and 70 percent of the largest companies in the world now have a benchmarking process in place. It is similar to Tom Peters's concept of model innovation. It involves ceasing to be afraid of one's competitors and taking time to learn from them — if not in terms of an exact product then at least in terms of how to do things. Robert Camp, a seventeen-year veteran of Xerox, wrote *Benchmarking: The Search for Industry's Best Practices That Lead to Superior Performance* in 1989. Benchmarking involves analyzing and adapting the methods of other companies. Thus, Motorola learned from Domino's Pizza how to shorten the time between receipt of an order for a cellular phone and its actual delivery. Though it is criticized as simply playing catch-up ball with innovators, benchmarking is more than that. In the corporate world, leaders are crossing disciplines and product lines more to learn principles and strategies of excellence and innovation from each other. Some say that on the emerging scene of global economics and trade, not to benchmark will mean the failure of some companies.

Benchmarking is a way of managing change. Xerox has been the chief advocate and teacher of benchmarking. What led Xerox into benchmarking was survival. It learned that the Japanese could make equally good copiers for less money. Not to study the Japanese would have meant death for Xerox.

Corporate friends tell me that often people in a company, especially its leaders, are shocked by the difference between what they consider their peak performance and what "the best" truly is. This phenomenon of the corporate world points to how complacent all organizations can become. Fred Bentzel, a specialist at Alcoa, says there is actually a period of *denial* in benchmarking, as companies compare themselves with what other, truly excellent companies have achieved. Again, benchmarking is not just product comparison or analysis of direct competition. When a company wants to improve an aspect of its operation, it can benchmark in any area. First Chicago Bank has benchmarked airlines to discern how better to handle long lines. Often there is great value in going outside one's own industry to benchmark. Alcoa Aluminum, for example, has benchmarked Dow Chemical, DuPont, and Hercules, Inc., for safety, General Electric for its approach to management. Alcoa has benchmarked eerox, Motorola, Hewlett-Packard, and TriNova for skills in benchmarking.

To initiate benchmarking in the corporate world is no easy task. Most experts say the chief obstacle to starting or succeeding in benchmarking is fear. Benchmarking depends a great deal on how it is imagined. If it is seen as a process of retroactive evaluation to make a scapegoat of someone or to criticize a past practice, it raises a lot of fear. It needs to be presented as a positive process of moving toward excellence. It is consoling to hear that not just church people — leaders, personnel, and congregations — but also people in the corporate world find it difficult to break routine and to be innovative.

Robert Camp says that the most difficult part of benchmarking is convincing company managers and workers that there are organizations out there better than they are. Overcoming myopia and organizational barriers to improvement can be very difficult. Camp says the most important part of the benchmarking process is preparation. Naming, prioritizing, and documenting the areas to be benchmarked are critical for good results. Camp says benchmarking always seeks two goals: to study and appropriate *the best* practices that are relevant to a given corporate body, and to provide customer satisfaction. Customer satisfaction is an ongoing pursuit. And an organization has to decide whether it will settle for minimum customer satisfaction or exceed it — sometimes at great cost. The same challenge lies before parishes that seek excellence in responding to parishioners' needs.

Alcoa (Aluminum Company of America) has a pamphlet describing the steps that it takes in benchmarking. I present those steps in the hopes that pastoral leaders can adapt them for benchmarking in pastoral ministry.

1. *Deciding what to benchmark*. Is the proposed topic important to customers [substitute *parishioners*]? Is the topic consistent with Alcoa's [the parish's] mission and values? This first step results in a purpose statement describing the topic to be benchmarked and some of the activities of the benchmarking team.

2. *Planning the benchmarking project*. A team leader is chosen, who is responsible for seeing that the project is successfully completed. This leader should be granted authority to recommend changes in processes and services based on emerging benchmarking information. The team's first task is to refine the benchmarking purpose statement by answering questions like these:

   • Who are the customers [group of parishioners] for study?

   • What is the scope of the study?

   • What aspects, characteristics will be measured?

   • What information about the topic is readily available?

   The team presents to the project sponsor [staff, parish council] all the information gathered up to this point. If the sponsor approves the proposal, the team moves on to step 3.

3. *Understanding your own performance*. This step engages in self-study. The team examines strengths and weakness, assets and deficits relative to the topic. The team discerns which behaviors seem vital to maintain and which ought to be altered or discontinued. Already at this stage, discussion can lead toward more excellent ways of behaving relative to the topic.

4. *Studying others*. The team:

   • identifies benchmarking candidates relative to the topic being studied;

   • then narrows that list to just a few candidates;

   • generates relevant general and specific questions;

   • decides how to get the questions answered;

   • then performs the study.

   During this step care must be given to ethical and legal issues.

5. *Using the findings*. The team returns to the sponsor [staff, council], reports the findings, and works together with the sponsor in determining how the findings can best be used. Consideration is given to many different parts of the organization and how the findings may benefit or be used by them.

Paul O'Neil, CEO of Alcoa says, "We want to benchmark everything we do against the best in the world."

In describing benchmarking to a group of diocesan priests and deacons recently, I used Willowcreek Community Church as an example of an excellent congregation. One priest earnestly asked, "Are you suggesting we take on all the trappings of an evangelical megachurch?" I responded, no. If benchmarking is done for parish life, one parish does not just replicate the organizations and style of another. Rather a parish decides what parts of parish life it wants to benchmark and then looks to other parishes that are excellent in that particular part of parish life. Thus, a parish might study Willowcreek for its great skills in hospitality and congregational, person-to-person reach-out. But the same parish might benchmark Bethel Lutheran for its ability to respond to real human needs and look to St. James in Arlington Heights for benchmarking in small communities, or St. John Neumann in St. Charles for excellence in youth ministry. For each aspect of parish life being benchmarked, the parish should probably study several models.

This book has been an attempt to start parishes in the process of benchmarking toward excellence. Benchmarking, along with pastoral alliances for excellence, could awaken "the sleeping giant" that George Gallup once spoke of in describing the Roman Catholic Church.

# EPILOGUE

# A Pastoral Alliance
# for Excellence in Evangelization

Manchester, New Hampshire; Tulsa, Oklahoma, Youngstown, Ohio; Cleveland Ohio; St. John's, Antigua, West Indies — these are among the many dioceses I have worked with in recent years to generate diocesan plans for evangelization. Since evangelization is my life's work, I would like to close by advocating that dioceses throughout the world do creative model innovation and generate pastoral alliances for excellence in evangelization. The following is a proposed plan, with ideas from some of the above dioceses, my own experience, and elsewhere. In speaking here of a pastoral alliance I am speaking very broadly. I am proposing that if evangelization is going to become more than just a "mouthed episcopal priority," and rather a true pastoral priority, diocesan agencies, under the direction of the ordinary, must work together. In turn, "downtown" must serve as consultants and facilitators for deaneries, vicariates, and clusters of parishes. Within a parish, the many different organizations and ministries will need to converge for a common mission. Some key elements in such a diocesan plan would look like this.

## Year One

*Fall:*

Education and consciousness raising of clergy and staff are done on vicariate, deanery, and cluster levels. A wholistic vision of evange-

123

lization is shared: re-evangelization of active members, reconciliation with alienated members, reach-out to the unchurched, more creative use of media, evangelization of families, evangelization of youth and young adults. Statistics regarding the local pastoral scene as well as emerging societal trends and evangelical needs are included here.

*Winter/Spring:*

The above evolving vision is transferred to the assembly, or active membership, through adult education, homilies, printed materials, etc. Emphasis is placed on the importance of the assembly and the individual as the most effective agents of evangelization.

*Summer:*

Preparation of materials for year two.

## Year Two

*Fall:*

A diocesan convention is held, perhaps entitled "Jesus Day — The Third Millennium: Evangelizing the Unchurched, the Alienated, and Ourselves." Speakers can be brought in for the large group sessions and practical workshops.

*Winter/Spring:*

A series of missions and revivals are held at pivotal churches with the theme "The Call to Conversion and Evangelization." The ordinary closes the series with a radio broadcast and homily for all the diocese.

*Spring/Summer:*

Each parish produces an inexpensive brochure introducing the neighborhood to the parish and the Catholic Church in general. Special mention should be made about welcoming those who have become inactive or alienated. Invitations can be included to quarterly open houses for the unchurched and the alienated. This marks the beginnings of a reach-out program. A team of trained parishioners canvas the neighborhood, dropping off the brochure at each home in the area.

## Year Three

*Fall:*

Quarterly nights of welcome and open house begin, at which the un-churched and alienated can begin dealing with their hurts and ask questions. These open houses can be jointly sponsored by neighboring parishes. Names, addresses, and phone numbers are retained for follow-up ministry. Good reading material is sent regularly to the very interested (e.g., *Information from...* [Paulist Press] or the diocesan newspaper).

*Lent: A Call to All Catholics: Remember, Return, Re-birth*

Special small group meetings are held in homes or at the parish site. Hopefully these small Lenten groups continue in some cases as small Christian communities. Necessary materials can be produced by agencies like Evangelization, Religious Education, Worship, Family Life, and Social Justice and by parishes working together.

Special parishes are singled out as sites for multiple opportunities for the sacrament of reconciliation.

*Easter-Pentecost: "The Fifty Days"*

The Office for Worship aids parishes in celebrating Resurrection for the full Easter season. During this period home visits or telephone evangelization of all in the parish neighborhood — active, inactive, unchurched — is carried out together with continued reach-out to those who have attended evenings of welcome and homecoming.

*Spring/Summer*

The Order of Initiation is fully implemented in all parishes, together with "Re-Membering Church," Alienated Catholics Anonymous, "Once a Catholic," or some adapted process of reconciliation for those who are alienated but returning to the church.

### End of Year Three

An event in the style of a Billy Graham crusade is held in a large gathering place or stadium, with all parishes represented. A suggested theme: "A Church in Mission."

As the above plan is adapted and implemented, parallel efforts should be engaged in for:

- adolescents
- young adults
- racial and ethnic subgroups
- grade-school children and their families in parochial school or religious education programs.

After three years a full evaluation ought to be done, discerning new learnings and shaping evangelization efforts for the future. Special attention should be given to emerging pastoral priorities to determine how the diocese and parishes will allocate attention, resources, and personnel in the future. All should be done in a spirit of collaborative interdependence. All the various pieces of diocesan life should converge on the one mission.

# Suggested Readings

CHAPTER ONE

Covey, Stephen. *Principle Centered Leadership*. New York: Simon & Schuster, 1989.
———. *The Seven Habits of Highly Effective People*. New York: Simon & Schuster, 1991.
Peters, Tom, and Nancy Austin. *A Passion for Excellence*. New York: Alfred A. Knopf, 1985.
Peters, Tom, with Robert Waterman. *In Search of Excellence*. New York: Alfred A. Knopf, 1982.
———. *Thriving on Chaos*. New York: Alfred A. Knopf, 1987.
Schaef, Ann Wilson, and Diane Fassell. *When Society Becomes an Addict*. San Francisco: Harper & Row, 1987.
———. *The Addictive Organization*. San Francisco: Harper & Row, 1988.

CHAPTER TWO

Brennan, Patrick J. *The Evangelizing Parish*. Allen, Tex.: Tabor Publishing, 1987.
Crosby, Michael. *The Dysfunctional Church*. Notre Dame: Ave Maria Press, 1991.
Donovan, Vincent. *The Church in the Midst of Creation*. Maryknoll, N.Y.: Orbis Books, 1989.
Fowler, James. *Weaving the New Creation: Stages of Faith and the Public Church*. San Francisco: Harper & Row, 1991.
National Conference of Catholic Bishops. *A Family Perspective in Church and Society*. Washington, D.C.: United States Catholic Conference, 1987.
———. *Putting Children and Families First — A Challenge for Our Church, Nation and World*. Washington, D.C.: United States Catholic Conference, 1991.

## CHAPTER THREE

Callahan, Kennon. *Effective Church Leadership*. San Francisco: Harper & Row, 1990.

Elkind, David. *All Grown Up and No Place to Go*. Reading, Mass.: Addison-Wesley, 1984.

Lincoln, C. Eric, and Laurence H. Mamiya. *The Black Church in the African American Experience*. Durham, N.C.: Duke University Press, 1990.

Sims, Rose. *New Life from Dying Churches*. Wilmore, Ky.: Bristol Books, 1989.

## CHAPTER FOUR

Deck, Allan Figueroa. *The Second Wave*. Mahwah, N.J.: Paulist Press, 1989.

## CHAPTER FIVE

Schaller, Lyle. *Growing Pains*. Nashville: Abingdon Press, 1983.

## CHAPTER SIX

Baranowski, Arthur C. *Creating Small Faith Communities*. Cincinnati: St. Anthony Messenger Press, 1988.

Baranowski, Arthur C., with Kathleen M. O'Reilly and Carrie M. Prio. *Praying Alone and Together*. Cincinnati: St. Anthony Messenger Press, 1988.

Brennan, Patrick J. *Re-Imagining the Parish*. New York: Crossroad, 1990.

## CHAPTER SEVEN

Guzie, Tad. *The Book of Sacramental Basics*. Ramsey, N.J.: Paulist Press, 1981.

Morris, Thomas. *RCIA: Transforming the Church*. Mahwah, N.J.: Paulist Press, 1989.

## CHAPTER EIGHT

Brennan, Patrick, and Dawn Mayer. *Reaching Out*. Cincinnati: St. Anthony Messenger Press, 1990.

## CHAPTER NINE

Brennan, Patrick. *The Evangelizing Parish*. Allen, Tex.: Tabor Publishing, 1987.

Cook, Paul, and Judith Zeiler. *Neighborhood Ministry Basics: A No-Nonsense Guide.* Washington, D.C.: Pastoral Press, 1986.

CHAPTER TEN

Bishops of Alta Baja, California. *A Pastoral Response to Proselytism.* March 1990.

National Conference of Catholic Bishops. *The National Plan for Hispanic Ministry.* Washington, D.C.: United States Catholic Conference, 1987.

Schwartz, Robert. *Servant Leaders of the People of God.* Mahwah, N.J.: Paulist Press, 1989.

Sofield, Loughlan, and Carroll Juliano. *Collaborative Ministry — Skills and Guidelines.* Notre Dame: Ave Maria Press, 1987.

CHAPTER ELEVEN

International Commission on English in the Liturgy and the Bishops' Committee on Liturgy. *The Rite of Christian Initiation of Adults.* Chicago: Liturgy Training Publications, 1988.

Morris, Thomas H. *Walking Together in Faith.* Mahwah, N.J.: Paulist Press, 1992.

CHAPTER TWELVE

Brennan, Patrick. *Penance and Reconciliation.* Chicago: Thomas More Press, 1986.

———. *The Reconciling Parish.* Allen, Tex.: Tabor Publishing, 1990.

Dallen, James. *The Reconciling Community.* New York: Pueblo Publishing Co., 1986.

CHAPTER THIRTEEN

Parks, Sharon. *The Critical Years.* San Francisco: Harper & Row, 1986.

CHAPTER FOURTEEN

Hoge, Dean. *Future of Catholic Leadership.* Kansas City, Mo.: Sheed and Ward, 1987.

CHAPTER FIFTEEN

Coles, Robert. *The Spiritual Life of Children.* Boston, Mass.: Houghton Mifflin Co., 1990.

Duggan, Robert, and Maureen Kelly. *The Christian Initiation of Children: Hope for the Future.* Mahwah, N.J.: Paulist Press, 1991.

Pfeiffer, Most Rev. Michael. "The Family and the Kingdom of God," in *Origins* no. 17 (February 25, 1988). National Catholic News Service, Washington, D.C.

CHAPTER SEVENTEEN

Camp, Robert. *Benchmarking: The Search for Industry's Best Practices That Lead to Superior Performance.* White Plains, N.Y.: Quality Resources, 1989.